The quest  common.
behind sor
endlessly do

this, I add a postscript to Paula's story, found in the NIV of Romans 8:28 "We know that in all things God works...". Despite the chaos, hurt, pain, and endless questions, God brought a beautiful soul into this world, whom we know as Paula. I highly recommend you read *Perfectly Imperfect* and explore how her personal journey, along with the insightful strategies she imparts, can empower you to cultivate a deeper trust in God.

Thetus Tenney, author, speaker, and
founder of World Network of Prayer

Though younger by quite a few years, Paula is one of my greatest teachers. I marvel at her ability to square off with barriers and pain and make them useful. It cost her a fortune to build her intriguing life. Now, she shares it—luring us into her 'ain't no mountain high enough' mindset. That's so Paula! (Beware! Excuses are pathetic after this read.)

Mickey Mangun, mickeymangun.com,
mangunmoments.com
founder and president of SEVEN Ministries,
recording artist

Paula has dedicated her life to creating a "purpose from the pain." The scars of the past have not defined her; rather, she has used them as a testimony of God's sustainability and strength through life's storms. Her faith, wisdom, dedication to healing, and true love for people can be felt in every line of this book. *Perfectly Imperfect* is a beautiful gift of encouragement and healing for us all.

Rhea Cooper, PhD, LPC-S, RPT, NCC

Paula is an inspiration and real-life hero to so many, including me. Throughout her life, in the face of overwhelming odds, she has demonstrated what faithfulness to the Lord is supposed to look like. She continues to be a beautiful example of what the Lord can do with a life fully surrendered to Him.

Valerie Hill, M.A., CRC
Executive Director of LifeSync Solutions,
Family Pastor Bethesda Church | Prairieville, Louisiana

Perfectly Imperfect will captivate you and move you to your core. It's not just a call to action, but a perfectly imperfect recipe of wisdom and life lessons that Paula so graciously shares with us. In Paula's words, if you are in the "land of the hurting," rest assure when you begin to flip the script and allow God to heal you from the inside out, your "land of the healing" is promised.

Vera Holloway, counselor, speaker,
and author of Your Second Chapter

Perfectly Imperfect is a must-read for those with painful pasts seeking a flourishing future. Through the author's story, discover the power of God's love and mercy to heal past wounds. This book empowers you to choose healing over hiding, showing you how to find beauty in imperfection and secure a brighter future. Paula's honesty and vulnerability make her an inspiring guide. You'll realize that flaws don't hinder making a difference or recognizing your inherent worth.

Angela Manning, child of God, avid reader, and life-long learner

It's rare to meet someone who has suffered stunning setbacks from the start and yet has decided to run to the finish with optimism, class, and grace. The gripping saga of Paula's overcoming life will have you shedding tears on one page and brimming with hope and confidence on the next. You won't be able to put it down, and it will definitely help you step into the place of those who have overcome and now live a life of full joy!

Madonna Massey, recording artist, interior designer, and Dolly to the greatest grandson, Weston Blue

From victim to victor, Paula has written a book that will inspire and challenge you. This is a powerful testament of God's love at work in our lives—even in the darkest of times. As you read *Perfectly Imperfect*, you will believe again that God is the "author and finisher" of not just your faith, but your story.

Hollie Nesmith, MA, English Literature

In *Perfectly Imperfect*, Paula embodies the essence of transformation. Open your heart and allow God to heal your soul as you immerse yourself in the captivating story of Paula's life. Through her journey, she has transcended her 'scars' to emerge as a powerful woman, a beautiful reflection of Jesus Christ. Prepare to be forever changed.

Janet Neyland, Christian education pastor, author, and interior designer

Paula's book, *Perfectly Imperfect*, will renew your faith and hope that God is never failing. As you read her life's testimony, you'll be reminded that God is always relentless with Love and Grace, to show us His beauty in our brokenness. If you want to be encouraged in your Spirit, *Perfectly Imperfect* will inspire you to put your trust once again in a God that sees and in time makes a way when there seems to be no hope.

Shelly Ralston, First Lady
First Pentecostal Church | Lake Charles, LA

Paula, a delightful soul, has written an overcoming story that will leave you full of hope for your own life experiences. Through *Perfectly Imperfect*, Paula equips us with the tools we need to reclaim our futures. A magnificent masterpiece!

Charidy Stanley, First Lady
New Life Church | Garland, TX

In *Perfectly Imperfect*, my dear friend Paula LeJeune shares her unfiltered and deeply moving journey of overcoming a traumatic past to find solace in God's love. Through her powerful story of forgiveness and resilience, Paula offers hope and encouragement to those navigating their own struggles. This book is a testament to the transformative power of God's presence and His enduring grace. A must-read for anyone seeking healing and redemption.

Jeana Weidner, First Lady
The Church of Pentecost | Ball, LA

Perfectly
Imperfect

Perfectly Imperfect

Flipping the Script on Scars

PAULA LEJEUNE

The various versions of Biblical scripture references have been used for clarity of meaning and appear in alphabetical order.

Scripture quotations marked AMP are taken from the Amplified® Bible, Copyright © 2015 by The Lockman Foundation. Used by permission. www.Lockman.org

Scripture quotations marked ESV® are taken from The Holy Bible, English Standard Version®, copyright © 2001 by Crossway, a publishing ministry of Good News Publishers. Used by permission. All rights reserved.

King James Version, (KJV)

New International Version (NIV) Scriptures are taken from The Holy Bible, New International Version®, NIV®. Copyright © 1973, 1978, 1984, 2011 by Biblica, Inc.® Used by permission. All rights reserved worldwide. The "NIV" and "New International Version" are trademarks registered in the United States Patent and Trademark Office by Biblica, Inc.®

New King James Version (NKJV) Scriptures are taken from the New King James Version®. Copyright © 1982 by Thomas Nelson. Used by permission. All rights reserved.

New Living Translation (NLT) Scriptures are taken from the Holy Bible, New Living Translation, copyright © 1996, 2004, 2015 by Tyndale House Foundation. Used by permission of Tyndale House Publishers, Inc., Carol Stream, Illinois 60188. All rights reserved.

Scripture quotations marked MSG are taken from *THE MESSAGE*, copyright © 1993, 2002, 2018 by Eugene H. Peterson. Used by permission of NavPress. All rights reserved. Represented by Tyndale House Publishers.

Any internet addresses (websites, blogs, etc.), phone numbers or company or product information printed in this book are offered as a resource. They are not intended in any way to be or imply an endorsement by The People Mover, nor does The People Mover vouch for the contents of these sites and numbers for the life of this book.

Cover design & interior illustrations: *Natalie Trahan*
Formatter: *Dallas Hodge, dalhodge56@gmail.com*
Interior design consulting: *Alyssa G. Bruce, alyssagbruce@gmail.com*
Publication consulting: *The Write Perspective, cher@thewriteperspective.net*
Publisher: *The People Mover, publications@thepeoplemover.us*

To Clifton,
the prince who saw past my external scars so well,
I don't see them anymore.
You had no idea of the internal ones.
Thank you for treating me right
when I treated you wrong.
Your patience and unwavering love
gave me the time and consistency
I needed to heal.
I love you.

Script Elements

PREVIEW

More than twenty physical scars decorate my five-foot one inch frame. Over half of them remain visible in normal clothing. I've spent much of my life focusing on them in private and trying to hide them in public.

The *Oxford English Dictionary* says, "A scar is a mark left on the skin or within the body tissue where a wound, burn, or sore has not healed completely, and fibrous connective tissue has developed." (Oxford English Dictionary 2016:Online)

But those are not the scars this book is about. This book is about that dictionary's second definition of the word, scar. It reads, "A lasting effect of grief, fear, or other emotion left on a person's character by a traumatic experience."

I have no clue how many of those trauma scars exist. Many of those wounds were reopened repeatedly until the scar tissue built up and threatened to suffocate my future. I didn't ask for them, they chose me. But it was up to me to deal with them.

In the beginning, those scars (both external and internal) were my justifications for poor choices, behavior, and mistakes. But as I matured, I learned that when I blamed others for my failures, I put the power to succeed in their hands. When I began to take responsibility for my actions, I reclaimed my future.

The hard purpose of Christ's mission would leave Him with "necessary scars." Before enduring the pain He knew was coming, He asked for a detour of His destiny. But afterward, the scars became a trophy of triumph that silenced the doubters. His scars were the proof of our purchased salvation. Their existence instilled hope in His believers.

The repercussions of my birth dictated that if I were to survive, scars had to be created. These were "necessary scars." It was up to me to discover the hope that lay beyond them.

We question God's will in our lives when pain is involved. But scars are proof to others that the pain existed, and we survived. Scars are proof that we have crossed over from the "land of the hurting" to the "land of the healing." The bridge between these two locations is forgiveness.

I am favored. Not because I am perfect but because God could trust me to make a difference in my imperfection. My face became a billboard of God's grace.

I had to decide what to do with that calling, that advertising, if you will. This book serves as a fulfillment of that decision.

As you turn the pages of this book, you will learn that it is possible to:

- Look brave while feeling broken.
- Find beauty in the blemish.
- Feel confident with your own compliments.

Luke 4:18–19 in the PKLV (Paula Kristine LeJeune Version) says, "The Spirit of the Lord has been on me since birth. He has anointed me to bring some good news to those who have lost hope. He has sent me to proclaim that your prison is not permanent, your vision will be restored, and show you that the keys to your future are in your hands. In His kingdom, the flawed are the favored."

Paula

This book delves into challenging topics such as violence, trauma, and mental health issues, which could be sensitive or triggering to certain readers. Reader discretion is advised. However, woven within these pages are narratives of resilience, perseverance, and the transformative influence of God's presence. We encourage readers to approach this material with an open mind and heart, recognizing the potential for growth and healing within its pages.

THE SETTING

The abundance of our lives is not determined by how long we live, but how well we live. Christ makes abundant life possible if we choose to live it now.

Barbara Brown Taylor

"For I know the plans I have for you," declares the Lord, "plans to prosper you and not to harm you, plans to give you hope and a future"

(Jeremiah 20:11 NIV).

1

CHOSEN TO DIE

The phone's shrill shattered the tranquility of a pre-dawn day in the spring of 1963. Startled, Janet hurriedly got out of bed and ran from her bedroom to the living room. With a hunch about the caller, Janet snatched the receiver from its resting place and said a quick hello. The voice on the other end confirmed it was the call she had been anticipating for several days.

"I think I'm in labor!" exclaimed the voice on the phone.

"How do you know?" Janet asked.

"I'm having contractions, and I can't sleep! Come over, and we'll drink a Coke and time them together."

"Let me grab some clothes, and I'll be there in a minute!" Janet squealed.

The voice on the phone was her cousin, Barbara, Bobbye to the family. Named after her grandmother, Barbara became Bobbye to avoid confusion.

Janet's parents and Bobbye's parents lived two houses apart. The two women had grown up together and were more like sisters than cousins.

Both were expecting children, and since Bobbye already had one child and was due before Janet, the two had become even closer. Janet was the novice, and Bobbye the expert. Filled with pregnancy advice and birthing expectations, the cousins filled their days discussing everything leading up to motherhood.

Bobbye was staying with her parents, Mac and Relia Sliman, in Kinder, Louisiana, because her husband, Wade, worked in another state, and she could no longer travel with him. Janet lived with her husband in Elton, a tiny town in Jefferson Davis Parish, Louisiana, but had decided to spend a few nights with her parents because she didn't want to miss this birth.

Hastily throwing on a dress, Janet brushed her teeth, dragged a comb through her hair, grabbed a light jacket, and drove the short distance to meet her cousin.

As she pulled into the driveway, Janet could make out Bobbye's silhouette leaning on the doorframe, waiting for her. Janet ran up the three steps to the porch and grabbed Bobbye's hand. A contraction was nearing the end, and Bobbye's red face indicated the pain level on that one was high. As soon as it lessened, the two entered the house and sat at the small table against the kitchen wall. Two Coke bottles were already out and opened, waiting for the women.

The pregnant women, one twenty years old and the other just over eighteen, giggled softly like schoolgirls as they drank the cold liquid and waited for the next wave of labor pains to begin.

Bobbye's parents were asleep in a bedroom just off the living room, and her nineteen-month-old daughter was sleeping soundly in the middle bedroom Bobbye shared with her ten-year-old sister.

Over the next couple of hours, the cousins shared stories and dreams for the future. Two women. Two pregnancies. Two babies whose mothers just knew would become close friends. Oblivious to how far off course their plans would go or how drastically altered the dreams for one of them would become, the two continued to plan their happily-ever-after lives, whispering and giggling as Bobbye's labor progressed.

When the contractions were consistently two to three minutes apart, Bobbye and Janet decided it was time to make the short trip to the hospital. Bobbye tiptoed into her mother's room to let her know. Relia mumbled something incoherent, then came fully awake. As she followed Bobbye into the living room, it was decided that she would stay behind with her older granddaughter until she was dressed and fed. She also promised to call Bobbye's in-laws and ask them to contact Wade.

Bobbye grabbed her shabby gray suitcase as Janet held the door for her. By the time Bobbye reached the car, another pain slammed through her, causing her to shriek and grab the roof of the vehicle for support. She leaned against the side of the car and, with her eyes closed, concentrated on breathing until the pain subsided. She opened her eyes, grinned, and announced, "My water just broke! We will need a towel."

Janet laughed as she rushed back into the house to grab a towel to protect her car seat. Within a couple of minutes, the two were on their way.

When they reached the hospital, Janet found a parking spot just a few steps from the front entrance. The hospital was small enough that almost any parking spot would have been considered "close." She jumped out, ran around the car, and opened Bobbye's door before the engine stopped squeaking out its mechanical song.

The hospital door swung open, and Nurse Agnes greeted the two with a hearty welcome. She had worked for Dr. Storer since he had begun his practice and knew almost everyone in town on a first-name basis. Bobbye and Janet referred to her as "Aunt Agnes."

Her wide smile and plump figure were a welcome sight to both women. Janet was grateful that someone else was taking charge of timing contractions. Bobbye had been hiding her pain behind a weak smile and was relieved that she could share her symptoms with Agnes. Her last pregnancy was textbook perfect, but this one had been difficult.

Over a dozen boils decorated Bobbye's skin, and as one would heal, another would erupt in a new place. Her pregnancy-induced craving was not for food but for dirt from the roads that ran along the fertile fields in Kings Farm, a small farming community west of Kinder.

Nurse Agnes ushered them into the tiny hospital room and bustled about getting Bobbye settled in for the delivery. She barked orders to another nurse as she grabbed a hospital gown and traded it for the suitcase.

She closed the curtain beside the bed and spoke gently and firmly. "You know the routine. Get this on," she said, "and lie on the table. Let's see if we can tell how soon this baby will debut."

A soft knock on the door heralded the entrance of Nell, one of the two women who worked in the front office. She was holding a clipboard containing the necessary paperwork to be signed. Agnes ordered her out until further notice. Nell grinned widely and exited, letting her words, "I'll be back in five!" trail behind her.

If Nurse Agnes believed in "patient privacy," it didn't appear to apply to her. Before Bobbye finished changing, Agnes appeared behind the curtain and began assessing. Her motherly tone of affirmation changed to one of concern as she caught sight of the boil sores and scars created by past boil eruptions.

"When did this start?" she questioned as she helped Bobbye onto the small hospital bed.

"I'm not sure. Maybe three or four months ago."

"Well, why didn't you come in and let us look at them sooner?" asked Agnes. Her once-friendly face now held a look of consternation.

Something wasn't right here. Agnes took note of the paleness of her patient's face and the staggered breathing and softened her voice. "Lie back, and let's get a look at your blood pressure."

Bobbye's temperature and blood pressure were above normal, but the numbers were insufficient to cause alarm. Agnes attributed the vital readings and the uneven breathing pattern to the fact that she was in labor. The rest of the preliminary examination revealed that her body was progressing quite nicely, and Aunt Agnes announced that this baby would appear before her shift ended.

Once Agnes was confident Bobbye was comfortably settled, she ordered Janet to stay put until she returned and left to grab more supplies and call the doctor. It wasn't long before Nell reappeared, obviously having gotten permission from Agnes. The three women visited with each other as Nell pointed and flipped pages, making sure Bobbye signed all the necessary paperwork.

The hands on the large, black-rimmed clock inched toward noon. By this time, the waiting room was full of family members. After all, this was Kinder. Everyone was either friends or kinfolk, or both. Bobbye's mother and grandmother and her mother- and father-in-law were there. Janet had gone back and forth from Bobbye's hospital room to the waiting area to give updates.

Each time she entered the waiting area, she asked if anyone had heard from Wade. Although Bobbye had yet to mention him since they arrived, Janet felt he should be there. He should have been at her side even though he wouldn't be allowed into the delivery room.

Nurse Agnes's and Dr. Storer's voices entered the room a second before they did. "And how are we feeling?"

Not waiting for a response, Agnes strapped the blood pressure cuff to Bobbye's arm and stuck a thermometer in her mouth. The crease on her forehead deepened when she saw the results: elevated blood pressure and a fever. Agnes wrote down the numbers and glanced at Bobbye. Her skin seemed paler than usual against her dark hair and eyes. Her cheeks were bright red, and her eyes watered as another contraction wracked her slim frame.

Pretending not to notice Agnes's concern, Dr. Storer chatted until the nurse finished her assessment. He told Bobbye to relax while he checked to see how her labor was progressing.

"This baby is anxious to meet its mama!" he grinned. "Let's move this party to the back!"

Janet stayed until they loaded Bobbye on a moveable bed. She hugged her for a long time and promised to be there when she returned with the family's newest member.

Dr. Storer wheeled her out, and Nurse Agnes walked beside the gurney, reassuringly stroking Bobbye's arm. She noticed how clammy it had become and made a mental note to inform the doctor when they reached the operating/delivery room.

The bright lights greeted the trio as the swinging doors closed behind them. Bobbye closed her eyes and groaned softly.

"It won't be much longer," encouraged Agnes. "Focus on your breathing."

Working together, the doctor and nurse slid Bobbye from the gurney onto the operating table. Although they had given her something for pain, the grimace on her face told them it wasn't having the needed effect.

Dr. Storer attached the stirrups to the bed, and Agnes guided Bobbye's feet into them. Agnes seemed to float around the room as she grabbed a pillow and blanket, making her patient as comfortable as possible. She leaned over, brushed her lips against Bobbye's temple, and whispered, "Everything is going to be alright. We're almost done."

The doctor sat on the low stool at the end of the bed and ordered Bobbye to push with the next contraction. She inhaled deeply, and a shaky moan filled the air as she exhaled and squeezed the sides of the table.

"Keep pushing! I see the head," coached Dr. Storer.

The baby's head was crowning and, after several pushes, still had not exited the birth canal. Doctor Storer grabbed forceps, gripped the baby's head, and paused, the room silent as everyone waited for the next contraction.

Suddenly, Bobbye stiffened and groaned as another wave of pain consumed her weak and feverish body. Doctor Storer pulled as Agnes repeated, "Push!" and just before the nurse felt that she would collapse, the baby slipped into the hands of the doctor.

A small sigh escaped from Bobbye's lips as she slid into unconsciousness. As he stared at the tiny human in his hands, the doctor was relieved that his patient was not alert. He would not have to answer any questions for the time being. He cursed and then whispered, "It's another girl."

Agnes watched the expressions on the doctor's face closely. She knew something was wrong but couldn't see much from her position behind Bobbye's head. Agnes eased her hands from under the young mother's back and walked around to look at the silent baby. Her eyes grew wide as her mind tried to understand what she was seeing.

The next few moments seemed like hours as the two moved about the room, checking their two patients' heartbeats, pulses, and erratic breathing. He did his best to clear the baby's airway, but no sound emerged from her tiny mouth. Her breathing became increasingly shallow, and her pulse faint. He massaged her chest and rubbed her back as long as possible before switching his attention to the mother. If there was a choice to be made as to who lived or died, the mother's life came first.

He turned to Nurse Agnes, who had not moved a muscle since coming to stand beside him. As he handed the baby to her, she sprang into action. Grabbing the towel from the surgical tray, she gently began wiping the blood and vernix, commonly called birthing custard, from the tiny, unmoving human. Agnes, too, rubbed the baby's chest and used a bulb to suction mucus from the infant's mouth.

The room vibrated with the frenzied movements of the doctor and nurse, employing every skill in their arsenal to rescue the two females. Neither spoke, but their eyes met every few seconds, looking for relief in the face of the other and finding none.

Agnes wrapped the infant tightly, silently pleading with her to breathe. Watching the tiny eyelids, with her outrageously full lashes too long for those paper-thin eye coverings, Aunt Agnes silently coaxed that baby to move. Agnes knew her words were useless to someone she suspected was not long for this life. Using the stimulation of her hands to encourage some fight into the tiny body, Agnes continued her silent support, hoping for some show, some sign, of life. Even a slight sigh would have been promising. Nevertheless, she saw no indication of life.

With heavy steps and a heavier heart, Agnes left the infant's side and walked to the operating table. Bobbye's pulse and blood pressure were lowering into a normal range, and her breathing was less erratic. Though Bobbye made sounds, her eyes remained shut as though silently protesting the reality she somehow knew was awaiting her.

Dr. Storer and Nurse Agnes spoke reassuringly, their voices not betraying how little confidence they felt since seeing the newborn. The doctor instructed Agnes to put the baby out of sight before the mother regained consciousness.

Knowing she needed her rest to recover, as well as to absorb the news he dreaded giving her, he administered a sedative into Bobbye's IV. He watched as her furrowed brow smoothed out, and she fully relaxed, sleeping deeply for the first time in days.

He checked her vitals once more before making the agonizing walk over to the table where the baby lay. He must thoroughly examine the infant before filling out the medical reports.

As he began unwrapping the baby, he saw her eyelashes flutter and mouth open, although no sound came out. He placed two fingers on her chest and felt the slightest movements from her lungs that were miraculously working.

Agnes was still at Bobbye's side, and Dr. Storer waved his hands to get her attention. Holding in a scream he knew would wake the mother, he mouthed, "SHE'S ALIVE!"

With a frantic forward motion, he commanded the nurse to the table holding the newborn. While they had been frantically focused on making sure this mother lived, the tiny newborn they left for dead had refused to give up.

Agnes's feet barely touched the floor as she raced to Doctor Storer's side. The infant's eyes opened and closed, and a long-overdue wail pierced the room's silence. It stopped almost as quickly as it began, and the two medical professionals, in unison, worked quickly to get the baby cleaned and rewrapped to meet the family.

But before joining the family, the medical team of two needed a plan.

———

They decided that Nurse Agnes would remain in the back with the baby, and another nurse would help the doctor move Bobbye back to her private room. Once he had safely transferred his patient from the operating table to the gurney and back into her bed, Dr. Storer made his way to the waiting area. As he walked, he mentally wrote and rewrote what he needed to say. Nothing in his medical training had prepared him for this moment.

Pushing open the door, he announced with forced exuberance, "It's another girl!" Raising his voice above the cheers and clapping, he instructed, "Now, I need you all to sit." There were no arguments; everyone found a place and faced him, eager for the update.

"First, both Bobbye and the baby are stable. I gave Bobbye medicine to help her sleep for a couple of hours. While she is sleeping, I will allow you to visit the baby, but I have to prepare you for what you see."

You could have heard a pin drop as they waited in fear-tinged puzzlement for his explanation.

"The baby has a growth attached to her chin and neck. It appears to have been another fetus that did not survive. Due to the size of the fetus's doll-like hands and feet, I'm estimating her death to have occurred between the end of the first trimester and the beginning of the second. The death of the second fetus explains the numerous boils present throughout Bobbye's body. The attached fetus also has a head full of dark hair, much like the baby's. At first glance, it looks like the baby has a beard, but as you get closer, you will make out the other features," he explained kindly but efficiently.

He paused and took a deep breath, giving everyone time to absorb the information. The family began bombarding him with questions. They knew the hospital was small and had limited capabilities. What was next? Where would the baby go to get help? What was the likelihood of survival? Of a normal life?

Dr. Storer raised his hand to silence them and said, "I don't know. I have some phone calls to make, and when Bobbye wakes up, we will make decisions together."

"In the meantime, two of you at a time can join Agnes in the back and greet your newest family member."

Bobbye's mother, Relia, and grandmother, Barbara, were the first to go back. They returned to the waiting area about fifteen minutes later to allow Wade's parents to take their place. It was evident both had been crying. Wade had still to make an appearance at the hospital.

Janet began firing questions at them as she waited her turn. She was devastated for her cousin. Things were not supposed to turn out like this today. How would Bobbye take the news? Could she handle the information that her second child was not "normal"?

With wide eyes, she placed her hands on her pregnant belly. Her brow furrowed as she wondered if something might be wrong with her baby too. But she stopped the words before they exited her mouth. She needed to get control of her emotions before Bobbye awoke. Her cousin needed her, and Janet was determined to be there.

After Janet took her turn in the back with Nurse Agnes and the baby, she asked if she could go and sit with Bobbye until she woke up. She needed to be there with her friend when she got the news. With Nurse Agnes's permission and a promise to eat a snack from the nurses' station, Janet assumed her post in a chair at Bobbye's bedside.

She watched the rhythmic movement of Bobbye's chest until she, too, fell asleep. When she heard someone calling her name, she was instantly alert. Bobbye was awake.

The nurse was already at her side, checking her vitals and trying to calm her down.

"Where's my baby?" Bobbye demanded.

The nurse looked helplessly at Janet, not knowing what to say. Janet ordered Bobbye to scoot over and crawled into the hospital bed with her. She asked the nurse to get Agnes and the baby and began to prepare her friend for what she was about to see.

As Janet explained, tears welled up in Bobbye's eyes. "It's not as bad as you think," Janet reassured her. "Dr. Storer believes everything can be fixed."

They could hear the baby crying as Nurse Agnes came down the hall. She was a bit flustered, acknowledging the baby had been crying for quite some time.

"None of my tricks are working!" she agonized.

Janet took charge of the situation.

"Put the baby between us."

Once settled securely between the two women, the newborn became silent. With an amazed gaze, Janet reverently watched Bobbye get acquainted with her new baby.

"What do you want to name her?" asked Janet.

"I wanted 'Paulette,' but Wade was so sure it would be a boy, we had settled on 'Paul.'"

"Why don't you name her Paula?" suggested Janet. "That's a good compromise since Wade isn't here, and we don't know when he will get home."

Bobbye nodded, too overcome with emotions to speak.

Several minutes later, still staring at her baby, she whispered, "Paula Kristine."

The rest of the day was a blur as family members came and went. Their comments were supportive while in the room, but she could hear them whispering to each other as soon as they cleared the doorway.

A fierce desire to protect this baby welled up inside of her. How would she shield her from stares and comments? She began with the next aunt, who entered the room carrying a camera. Bobbye shook her head vehemently, not allowing a single picture to be taken.

Late that evening, Dr. Storer made rounds and pulled up a chair at Bobbye's bed. He had been on the phone for several hours and had been able to secure a bed at New Orleans Charity Hospital. The surgeon who would head up the team assigned to Paula was a friend of Dr. Storer. He explained the need to move baby Paula to a different hospital, one better equipped to handle Paula's diverse medical conditions. He assured Bobbye of her baby's safety. Reluctantly, Bobbye agreed to the transfer.

Wade was still a no-show at the hospital; no one knew how to contact him. Bobbye could not make the four-hour trip to New Orleans for several days, so traveling with her baby was not an option. It was decided Janet, Relia, and Barbara would make the trip early the following morning with the fragile and unique child.

Bobbye spent one night with her daughter before having to say goodbye. It was a traumatic night for mother and baby. After unsuccessfully attempting to breastfeed, Bobbye called the night nurse for a bottle. Paula struggled to latch on to anything and cried intermittently during the long night. Neither mother nor child slept for more than an hour.

The next morning, as promised, the three women arrived to transport Paula to New Orleans. Bobbye delivered a long, hard kiss to her sweet baby's head. She closed her eyes as she inhaled the newborn's fragrance and moved her lips against her soft hair. Nurse Agnes had just come on duty and stood by patiently, waiting for permission to separate the baby from her mother. There were no dry eyes in the room.

The baby who was chosen to die had refused to do so. Her stubbornness would serve her well during the coming years.

2

WANTING TO DIE

Now I lay me down to sleep.
I pray the Lord my soul to keep.
And if I die before I wake,
I'll be at peace, make no mistake.

My earliest memories of Dad's abuse involved my oldest sister, Jonette. Some of the stories were told to me, and others I witnessed.

Jonette was the first child born in our family. When she was a baby, if her crying annoyed Dad, he would hold his hand over her mouth and nose while repeatedly yelling, "Shut up!" until she stopped. Sometimes, he didn't remove his hand until my mom began screaming because Jonette was turning blue. Long before her first birthday, if Dad said, "Shut up," Jonette stopped crying.

I'm not sure if that was his method for teaching the rest of us; I only know that none of us were crybabies. Early on, we all knew if we cried, it better be for a good reason, or Dad would give us "something to cry about."

Once, as a toddler, Jonette was playing in the yard. Dad asked her to bring him the water hose. She looked around, confused, which angered Dad. He yelled, "It's the thing you're standing on!"

Looking down, Jonette saw both her feet were in the grass. Bending over, she grabbed two handfuls of grass and brought them to him. Instead of laughing at her age-appropriate comprehension, he became enraged. Dad grabbed her arm and dragged her to the water hose, picked it up, and began beating her with it. When Mom started screaming, the beating abruptly ended.

After that event, Jonette would take a dramatic step over every water hose she saw. In her childlike understanding, the beating was due to her standing on the water hose. She would not make that mistake again.

———

When I was around four years old, I stepped on a board with nails sticking out, and one nail pierced deep into my heel. I yanked the nail out and ran into the house to clean the blood off, fearful that I would be in trouble for leaving a trail of blood behind me. I didn't dare to cry.

The moment she saw the blood, Jonette started screaming at the top of her lungs. My parents appeared at the door, and I ran past them while they tried to figure out what upset Jonette. I had cleaned up most of the blood before they figured out that I was hurt. Dad whipped six-year-old Jonette for screaming for "no reason."

Jonette, however, didn't learn her lesson about that habit of screaming for no reason.

———

I was twelve and playing outside with my sisters, Jonette and Trudy, and a neighborhood friend. My friend was riding her horse, and Jonette was seated behind her. Jonette was tightly holding a rope that was attached to a small red wagon. Trudy and I were passengers in the wagon. I held the long wagon handle between my knees and attempted to steer it as we rode down the street.

The wagon hit a pothole in the road and tumbled over. Trudy and I were thrown from the wagon, and my right knee slammed into a jagged piece of pavement, creating a wide gash in my skin.

I jumped up, assuring everyone I was okay, and felt the blood running down my leg. When I bent over to examine my knee, I could see the bone. I covered the opening with my right hand and limped down the road and into the house, trying to get to a bandage before my parents discovered that, as usual, I had "made a mess."

Once again, Jonette's voice was the siren that followed me, warning my parents that something was wrong. By the time Dad understood who was hurt, I was sitting on the edge of the bathtub with a rag over my knee, trying to figure out how to cover the wound. All the bandages we had were too small.

Dad told me how stupid I was for participating in such a dangerous activity. He made sure I knew that I had brought this pain on myself. Then he instructed Mom to get me to the emergency room while he "took care" of Jonette for crying "for no reason." The ER staff cleaned the wound, numbed the area, and stitched it up. Again, I did not cry. I knew firsthand the consequences of crying.

Somewhere around this time, Mom began having nightmares of Dad killing Jonette. Those nightmares became more frequent as we got older. When Mom would have one of her nightmares, she would go into Jonette's room and wake her to make sure she was okay. Occasionally, Dad would accompany her to see Jonette, and the three of them would sit in the kitchen and talk.

Mom would share the terrible dream, and Dad would promise not to hit us again. It didn't take long for him to break that promise. If something set him off, he reacted violently until his anger abated. When he was out of control, things got destroyed, someone got hurt, and we all prayed for death.

———

In the spring of 1979, we witnessed Dad nearly making Mom's nightmare a reality.

Jonette was a senior in high school, I was a sophomore, Trudy was a freshman, and Terri and Laura were in elementary school.

As usual, Dad had misplaced several things and had all of us running around wide eyed, searching every area of the house. As the minutes ticked by without any success, Dad began to yell. We were desperate to avoid him while digging through piles of papers, clothing, unorganized vanity drawers, cluttered closets, and overstuffed trash cans. No spot went untouched.

As Jonette left one room and headed to the next, she passed Dad in the hallway. Looking for an outlet for his anger, he decided she didn't appear to be taking the search seriously and ordered her to the living room located in the center of the house.

Our search was interrupted by Jonette's pleas for mercy, deadly screams, and the sound of his belt repeatedly hitting her body. With chills running down our spines, we raced toward those sounds, hoping Dad would stop once he saw the rest of us in the room.

He was in a blind rage and didn't seem to notice us as he continued to use the belt, his fists, and then, finally, his pointed cowboy boots. We were all screaming, and Jonette's wail pierced through the chaos as she screamed at Mom, "He's going to kill me, and it's going to be your fault!"

Her words seemed to snap Dad out of his rage. He stood motionless for a second, staring at her now silent and limp body. He released the belt and ran out of the room. We heard the back door slamming, then the quick follow of a screech as his car's tires screamed his exit.

We rushed to where she lay motionless on the floor, silently begging God to let her be alive. She survived, but our spirits did not. We were broken.

We knew what he was capable of, and I begged God to let us die swiftly and mercifully in some other manner. I did not want Dad to have the pleasure of seeing us die by his hand.

When he returned several days later, no one discussed it. We treated this incident like every other one, pretending it never happened.

───

Trudy took a speech class during her sophomore year at Welsh High School. A large part of the grade was the school play. Although they worked on the script during school hours, rehearsals were held in the evening.

On the afternoon of one of the practices, between school and the rehearsal, Trudy was helping Dad work on a motor. While Dad referred to each of us as "boy," he decided Trudy was the most masculine; therefore, she was often required to work on vehicles. She had learned almost all the tools and could lift heavy objects.

This day was special. Trudy was excited because Mom and Dad had agreed to allow her to ride to practice with a boy from school. Trudy had been talking about the play as she and Dad worked, and Dad interrupted, asking for a tool. While she was digging for the tool in his unorganized toolbox, Dad decided she was taking too much time. His belt came off in that familiar swish, and he began to beat her all over her body, avoiding her face. He always avoided our faces because they couldn't be covered to hide bruising.

As he hit her, he yelled that this would be the last time she had boys on her mind when he had more important things for her to do.

As she dressed for the evening rehearsal, Trudy picked out a long-sleeved sweater with a long skirt. She did her best to hide the belt marks. When the boy came to get Trudy and asked why she wore long sleeves on such a warm evening, Trudy claimed to be cold. She would be cold for several weeks until the marks healed.

———

Dad was often cruel to animals in front of us. Those times were messages of what he would do to us if we crossed him intentionally.

It was the summer after I graduated from high school, and Trudy had finished the eleventh grade. I was at work at the little accounting office in Welsh that my mom managed. Trudy and Dad had been working outside but stopped to eat lunch. As they entered the kitchen, Dad bent down to pet our new puppy, and the puppy snapped at him. Trudy watched in horror as Dad became immediately enraged and began beating the dog, not stopping until it lay limp. A slow movement in the dog's chest let the two of them know it was still alive.

Dad sent Trudy to get some rubber bands from her room and then wrapped the bands around the dog's mouth. He walked outside and laid the dog at the end of the driveway in the hot sun, making Trudy follow and watch. The heat index was just over 100°.

Dad then ordered Trudy back inside, where chores awaited her attention. Dad sat on the sofa with his Bible and waited.

An hour later, he called Trudy and said, "Go and see if that dog is still alive."

Trudy rushed out to where the dog lay and was grieved to see that its chest was still moving. Holding back tears, she went inside and reported, "He's still alive."

She continued cleaning and doing her best to keep her mind occupied until Dad called her to him again. "Go and see if that dog is still alive."

With heavy steps, she made her way to the lifeless animal at the end of the drive, praying that its misery was over. But the dog continued to breathe.

He repeated the order five more times. Each time, the puppy was still alive.

Just before dark, Dad ordered Trudy to go with him outside. When she realized they were headed to where the dog lay, she whispered a prayer that it would be dead, but God didn't answer her prayer.

Dad bent down to examine the animal and grunted in disgust that it was hanging on to life. He glanced at Trudy to make sure she was watching as he grabbed the dog with both his hands and twisted the dog's neck, ending its life.

Neither the dog nor Trudy made a sound.

Dad convinced us all, Mom included, that if we ever tried to leave or if we ever told anyone about anything he did, there would be a murder/suicide.

As I wrote these stories out, I realized what was more traumatic for us than the actual physical abuse was not knowing what we would "do wrong" in the future. None of us kids were rebellious or disrespectful. We truly wanted to please both of our parents. What angered Dad on one day, he either didn't notice or didn't respond the same on another day.

Had we been given a list of rules, we would have expected punishment for breaking them. But the mystery of rules unspoken and the inconsistency of the penalty for those infractions we did know about was torture.

My oldest sister worked for us when our daughters were young. She had a front-row seat to the relationship between Clifton and Eden and Eryn, our girls. Cliff was consistently affectionate and patient with both girls.

Anytime I stopped by the office with them, their arrival was the unspoken announcement that it was playtime. He would immediately stop working and scoop them up in his arms, evoking high-pitched screams and giggles. The noise level escalated and reverberated through the small offices. Jonette and I could not help but laugh with them.

One day, as she watched the girls race toward Clifton's office and listened for the familiar, loving chaos, tears welled up in her eyes, and she looked at me and said, "Why couldn't God have given us a daddy like Cliff?" It was a question I had already asked Him, but He hadn't answered.

As a father, Clifton displayed the characteristics of a loving God who is kind, gentle, and ever ready to support and sustain His children. As kids, my sisters and I had never seen this in our dad. It was no wonder we had such a warped sense of the magnitude of God's love. It would be many years before I unwrapped the tough layers of a childhood that left me eager to escape, even if it meant dying.

3

CHOOSING TO LIVE

I spent twenty-five years in prison. During my incarceration,
I took courses in "How I Do Not Want to Live."

My dad was the pastor of our small church, and our family was wealth deficient. Problems between him and my mom, financial difficulties, and the stress of pastoring added to his uncontrolled temper. My sisters and I became the outlet for his frustration. Minor infractions often resulted in harsh consequences that left us bruised and battered.

With no income of our own and nowhere to go, we were prisoners. Dad was the warden.

But we could escape for a little while when we went to church. Dad's attention was focused on the congregation. Although he showed no mercy with how he spoke to us, he restrained himself from hitting us when others were present.

It was at church where I witnessed church members, whom I felt were living in their own prisons, respond differently to their circumstances.

33

One family consisted of a mom, a dad, and six boys. They seemed as poor as we were, if not poorer. They lived about twenty miles from the church. We had two services on Sundays, morning and evening. To save money on fuel, they would often pack sandwiches and water and spend their Sunday afternoons under the trees on the church property.

I was around nine years old when I met them. Their oldest son, who was in his twenties, had muscular dystrophy and was confined to a wheelchair. He had the sweetest disposition. I still remember his brothers roughly wheeling him into the church. He would smile and joke about his "nurses." I felt sorry for him, but I don't remember him ever feeling sorry for himself.

He was always smiling and humming. Occasionally, my dad would let him sing a solo during a service; most of the time, he sang the same song. It was an old song by recording artist Dottie Rambo called "Don't Take My Burdens or My Cross Away." He would belt out the lyrics, letting God know he didn't despise his circumstances. They were what kept him close to God.

I remember sitting in the front row and thinking I would be constantly asking God to take away my disease if I had muscular dystrophy. I wouldn't be singing, "Don't take it away." And I certainly wouldn't be smiling like he was!

Then, the mother of that family began having symptoms of a genetic disease similar to muscular dystrophy. Her body started having spasms, which affected the way she moved and walked. Her speech became slurred, making it difficult to understand her when she spoke. Eventually, she, too, became dependent on a wheelchair for mobility.

I felt so sorry for her. But, like her son, I don't remember her ever feeling sorry for herself. She also loved to sing, and my dad allowed her to participate in services.

Her favorite song was a Dottie Rambo song as well. I assumed they were so poor they only had one record. The title of her song was "I Just Came to Talk with You, Lord."

From the confines of her wheelchair, she sang about not praying for her needs but just wanting to talk with God.

Listening to her sing, I thought, *I know many things you need to be asking God for! For starters, how about a healthier body? You need God to take this disease away so you can take care of yourself and your children.*

But she remained positive. Even when her youngest son was diagnosed with muscular dystrophy, she never grew despondent. She and her husband remained steadfast in their faith and their attendance. She became a hero in my eyes.

I watched as her condition worsened to the point where she could barely hold her head up. Her smile, though, remained the same. Her voice became a whisper, but you could hear her singing if you got close.

She may have been in "prison," but she was definitely not a "prisoner"! Although this family would not have been considered successful by anyone's standards, they were successful in keeping peace in their hearts and minds.

An article from *Making Music Magazine* titled "Three Ways Singing Makes You Healthier" by Uche Ibe claims, "Singing is a natural antidepressant. When you sing, your body releases endorphins—chemicals that make you happy. So, the next time you feel down, break into your favorite song. Singing also helps in lowering your stress levels. When you are stressed, a hormone called cortisol in your body increases. Singing is found to reduce the level of cortisol in the body, easing the tension and helping you to relax." (Ibe n.d.)

Paul and Silas figured out how to escape prison long before *Music Magazine* and the health profession did. Their story is found in Acts 16 (NKJV). Here's the PKLJ summary.

Paul and Silas were traveling evangelists who had seen miracles, signs, and wonders. They were fulfilling the Great Commission, and doors opened for them to share the gospel.

One day, they were on their way to a prayer meeting, and a slave girl, a fortune-teller, began following them. The Bible records that her owners made a living from her "gift." As the evangelists walked through the streets, she began drawing attention to them by yelling, "These men are the servants of the Most High God, who proclaim to us the way of salvation."

She didn't just follow them for one day. Verse 18 says, "And this she did for MANY days.

"But Paul, greatly annoyed, turned and said to the spirit, 'I command you in the name of Jesus Christ to come out of her.' And he came out that very hour.

"But when her masters saw that their hope of profit was gone, they seized Paul and Silas and dragged them into the marketplace to the authorities. And they brought them to the magistrates and said, 'These men, being Jews, exceedingly trouble our city; and they teach customs which are not lawful for us, being Romans, to receive or observe.'"

The girl's masters were so convincing that the Scriptures claim that "the magistrates tore off their clothes and commanded them to be beaten with rods."

After they were beaten, they were thrown into prison, and the jailer "fastened their feet in the stocks."

If you can visualize this for a moment, Paul and Silas were doing good things. They were helping people. And their reward was to be beaten and thrown in jail! They are in pain, they can't get comfortable, they are wrongfully charged, and they have every right to throw a pity party.

Instead of doing this, verse 25 says, "But at midnight Paul and Silas were praying and singing hymns to God."

We all know the rest of the story. There was a great earthquake, the doors opened, and EVERYBODY'S chains were loosened.

I learned to sing. Singing became my antidepressant. I wish I could tell you that breaking into song fixed everything, and I never struggled again. It didn't. You will read accounts of my poor thinking and behavior throughout this book. Some of these stories are from my childhood, and some are from after marriage. The following story unfolded when I was fifty-five years old.

In July 2018, Clifton took a two-week motorcycle trip from Louisiana to the West Coast. He turned fifty earlier that year, and the trip was on his "bucket list."

Prior to his leaving, several people came to me and asked why I was allowing him to go on such a long motorcycle trip. I would reply that it was his dream and that I wasn't his mother. One woman in our church approached me and said she had a "funny feeling" about his trip. I never said a word to him about it and decided to list things I wanted to accomplish before he returned. This would keep me from dwelling on the negative things my mind quickly conjured up.

I did my best to put on a good face for him as he pulled out of our driveway. Whenever he called, I made a conscious effort to sound as cheerful as possible. I didn't want him to worry about me worrying. He deserved to enjoy his vacation. His phone calls were filled with sights and events, and I listened as I choked back tears caused by the fear that threatened to take hold of me.

Sleep was sometimes difficult until I knew he was safely at a hotel. Because he had gone to the Pacific Coast, he was in a different time zone, two hours behind me. If they rode until midnight, I didn't sleep until 2 a.m.

We have an app on our phones called Life 360 that allows me to check his location. This app helped put my mind at ease when worry and fear tried to creep in. I could look at Life 360, and if it said he was moving, I felt better. But if it said he had stopped, I would zoom in and see where he was. Sometimes, he would be at a gas station. Other times, he would be at a restaurant. I had peace as long as I could find him and know he was safe.

I was so proud of myself and was daily patting myself on the back at what a trooper I was...until Thursday afternoon on the return trip. Cliff had been making the long trek back home and was scheduled to be home early the next afternoon. The girls and I had been making plans for the "Welcome Home" reunion, and I was sitting at the snack bar in my kitchen working on a lesson to teach my class at church when my cell phone rang. The caller ID scrolled "Clifton LeJeune" across the screen.

Swiping right, I answered cheerily, "Well, hello, Clifton!"

Cliff's tone was serious as he reported, "Tim had a blowout. We are okay, but this is going to set us back a while."

I tried to be brave and optimistic, but after several phone calls and disappointments, I caved into the familiar pit of despair and self-pity. I put up bars around myself, creating a self-imposed prison.

I knew I was in trouble and tried to get out without help. I even spent time in my prayer closet, wailing to God about my predicament.

MY. PREDICAMENT.

My husband was sitting on the side of the interstate in New Mexico with his friend, who had a flat tire. It was JULY and well over 100°. Sitting in an air-conditioned house, I thought I had a predicament.

Looking for encouragement, I turned to my *Jesus Calling* devotional, and the words leaped from the page and hit me between the eyes. It read, "Bring Me all your feelings, even the ones you wish you didn't have. Fear and anxiety still plague you. Feelings per se are not sinful, but they can be temptations to sin. Blazing missiles of fear fly at you day and night; these attacks from the evil one come at you relentlessly. Use your shield of faith to extinguish those flaming arrows. Affirm your trust in Me, regardless of how you feel. If you persist, your feelings will eventually align with your faith.

"Do not hide from your fear or pretend it isn't there. Anxiety that you hide in the recesses of your heart will give birth to fear of fear: a monstrous stepchild. Bring your anxieties to the Light of My Presence, where we can deal with them together. Concentrate on trusting Me, and fearfulness will gradually lose its foothold within you." (Young 2004)

The steady stream of tears turned into sobs as I began telling God exactly how I felt and got as honest with Him as I could. That old "victim mentality" that I had wrestled with for so many years came rushing home at an alarming rate of speed. Instead of resisting, I had welcomed its gloomy covering.

I yelled at God, "It's just not fair! I have been a good wife, accepting that I would be 'flying solo' for a few days, and now those days will be longer. This is unfair, and I don't do well with unfair! Cliff should be on his way home! Not sitting on the side of the road waiting for assistance!"

When I stopped yelling, God began to speak and His words convicted me. "What are you focused on?"

As I knelt in silence and dug through my thoughts, I realized that I had been focused on all the "what-ifs" for his trip for days. What if he had an accident? What if he had a stroke or a heart attack? What if his friend had an accident? What if he went missing? What would I do without him?

For almost TWO WEEKS, I had been focused on my fears. It felt like I had been holding my breath for the past twelve days, and I was angry because I would have to continue holding it even longer.

I've read *Enemies of the Heart* by Andy Stanley (Stanley 2011) so many times I can almost quote it word for word. I know anger says, "You owe me," and something was being taken from me. It was my peace. But as I thought about it, I realized it was not being taken from me; I was handing it over. The professional devil was doing what he was a professional at; he was offering me fear and anxiety. And I was willingly trading my peace for it! How stupid is that?

Fear causes you to slip back into old mindsets. Negativity was the "safe space" I had crawled back into.

In his book, Andy says the remedy for anger is forgiveness. But first, I had to decide just who I was angry with. Who had stolen from me? As I processed my thoughts, I decided I was angry with a TIRE! A MOTORCYCLE TIRE! I needed to forgive the tire of failing to hold in the pressure and causing the delay in my husband's trip, and then I needed to quit acting like a child and move on! Life happens. No one was injured. No damage (other than a tire replacement) was done to the motorcycles. My husband was still coming home. I felt silly at how childish my thoughts had become.

I was mortified to find myself once again in a self-imposed prison of despair.

If the story in Acts 16 were about Paula instead of Paul, it probably wouldn't have included singing. It would have been described as a disturbing screech as I lashed out at God with, "REALLY? We were doing YOUR WORK! Is THIS the way You pay YOUR HELP? THIS IS SO UNFAIR!"

I am not proud that I am a professional pity party thrower. No one has ever hired me or wanted to attend my parties. They were always sold out anyway. That crowd of one filled the emotional space so tight it was standing room only and reeked of self-centeredness.

I'm unsure if Paul was thinking of his jailbreak incident or had encountered others like me when he wrote Philippians 4:4. His letter to the church in Philippi sounds repetitive when he writes, "Rejoice in the Lord always. Again, I will say, 'Rejoice'!"

I knew what I needed to do. I needed to sing. Paul and Silas had taught me. The family in our church had taught me.

Alone in my kitchen, I began to sing praises to God. In between songs, I began claiming aloud the promises of verse 6 of Philippians 4: "Be anxious for nothing, but in everything by prayer and supplication, with thanksgiving, let your requests be made known to God. And the peace of God, which surpasses all understanding, will guard your hearts and minds through Christ Jesus." (NKJV)

Within seconds, anger, fear, and anxiety melted away and left me with the peace that God intended for me to experience.

For a moment, I want to go back to the sentence in Acts 16:25, "…and the prisoners were listening to them."

My younger daughter, Eryn, lived at home during the infamous motorcycle trip. She was in the room with me during one of the frustrating phone calls. She watched as I struggled with my emotions. I knew that I had to get control of myself because my attitude affected hers. It also affected the environment of our home. At that moment, I was teaching her how to handle disappointment and adversity. My song had the potential to free everyone who was listening.

It didn't matter what I was going through or what prison I thought I was in; I could choose to break into song. So, I began to sing loudly because another "prisoner" was listening. I wanted her to learn how peace is recovered and restored.

Notice: the Bible did not say that Paul and Silas FELT like singing. It just tells at midnight, in their darkest hour, they sang. When I feel like a prisoner, I won't feel like singing. But if I sing, something will happen!

Perhaps that is why the Psalmist David talks about singing over one hundred times in the book of Psalms. He discovered one of the keys to unlocking your prison is in your song.

I lived in what I believed to be a prison until I left home at twenty-five years old. But it was up to me to decide if it was a "Death Sentence." I chose to sing.

THE TENSION

*The womb is a dark place where
you receive the nutrients to survive.*

*God always gives the best to those
who leave the choice with him.*

Jim Elliot

*This day I call the heavens and the earth
as witnesses against you
that I have set before you life and death,
blessings and curses.
Now choose life,
so that you and your children may live*

(Deuteronomy 30:19 NIV).

4

FACING THE FACTS

I was one day old when the Pediatric Intensive Care Unit at New Orleans Charity Hospital became my home for a few weeks. None of my family was allowed to stay with me. It would be a full week before any family member would see me again.

While the staff there made sure to care well for me, I was not cared for. "Spoiled" babies made for difficult patients, and strict instructions were given as to the length of time anyone could hold me.

A feeding tube was inserted directly into my stomach to allow tests and surgeries to be done on my mouth. That tube would remain for several months, and once removed, a three-inch scar would permanently decorate my stomach.

During the separation surgery, doctors discovered that my twin's tongue was attached to the floor of my mouth. Instead of removing it, they sewed the two together. My parents were warned that there was a high probability that I would never speak.

The tongue is a muscle, and controlling that muscle allows you to speak. There was no record of anyone mastering two tongues; thus, the reason for their prediction.

The outcome is I did learn to speak. My irrepressible sense of humor makes me add, but because I have two tongues, I must watch what I say twice as much as everyone else.

Muscles and salivary glands were intricately woven together in utero, making it difficult to tell which were mine and which belonged to my twin. So, I ended up with extra neck muscles and extra salivary glands.

Once successfully separated from the parts of my deceased twin, there was a gap where a chin should have been. My jawline stopped toward the front, leaving me with no bone structure for a gumline to form. I did not have bottom front teeth until I was nineteen years old.

The extra glands and the fact that I could not properly close my mouth caused saliva to run freely, soaking bandages covering fresh scars. As a result, healing was slow, and infections were frequent.

My parents faced the fact that I would require many surgeries as I grew. Doctors had a plan for some of those operations. Others would occur on demand.

The extra muscles in my neck kept the skin taut, making scar tissue thicken instead of flattening and relaxing. The large scars would prevent neck movement and pull my chin toward my chest. Those scars had to be removed repeatedly, only to form again at the point of the incisions.

Similar surgeries done on other patients were successful, but mine were deemed experimental because of the rareness of my condition. There was nothing ordinary about my circumstances.

By the time I was three, Dad had a decent job in Austin, Texas, and my parents purchased a little two-bedroom white house on top of a hill. Although I don't remember much of my life before I turned six, I remember this house. Dad and Mom occupied one bedroom, and my two sisters (at the time) and I shared the other. Jonette and Trudy would sleep in the same bed, but I had to sleep alone.

My parents located a plastic surgeon nearby, and he performed several surgeries, including a bone graft. He took a rib from the right side of my rib cage and created a chin for me. Within a short period, the bone graft became infected, and the infection worked its way through my scar. One evening, Mom was bathing me, and as she wiped my face, the skin separated, exposing the bone.

She rushed me to the hospital, where an emergency surgery was performed. Another piece of rib, this time from the left side of my chest, was used. Today, I have asymmetrical scars several inches long on my chest and a wire wrapped around that piece of rib in my chin.

When I awakened from this surgery, I was wearing a body cast that covered me from the top of my head to my waist. There was an opening for my face, the back of my hair, and my arms. This cast would be my "shirt" for the next few months until x-rays showed that the bone had grafted.

Because falling out of bed could be fatal for me, Mom set up a borrowed baby bed in the living room, where I would sleep for those months. I remember being embarrassed when we had guests, and they found out it was where I slept. I refused to lie in it if other people were present.

As I grew, my surgeon performed procedures necessary to accommodate my growth. By the time I was twenty-three years old, I had had almost thirty surgeries or medical procedures. In this chapter, I want to share the details of the last two reconstructive surgeries.

But first, I want to turn to a Scripture taped on the wall in my "war room" (which will be discussed in the next chapter). It is found in Psalm 51:10 (KJV) and reads, "Create in me a clean heart, O God; And renew a right spirit within me."

Before I elaborate on that Scripture, I want to go over the story before this psalm was written. The story is in the book 2 Samuel, the eleventh chapter. While I could copy the exact text from any version of the Bible, I've chosen to use parts of the story from the NKJV and inserted my version, the PKLV, the Paula Kristine LeJeune Version.

The chapter begins with, "It happened in the spring of the year, at the time when kings go out to battle, that David sent Joab and his servants with him, and all Israel; and they destroyed the people of Ammon and surrounded the city of Rabbah. But David decided to stay home."

"IT" happened. We aren't sure who wrote David's story. Some biblical scholars believe it was his pastor, Nathan. But the writer was trying to go back and figure out exactly where King David had gotten off track.

At the time this story occurred, David had seven wives. Spending time with them would have been a justifiable reason not to go to war. But we know that's not the case because one night (PKLV), he began scrolling through social media when he had trouble sleeping. A picture of his neighbor, Bathsheba, caught his attention, and he began stalking her account.

He knew her husband, Uriah, was in the military and was deployed. By the seductive nature of her photos, he recognized her need for attention.

David sent her a private message, and she responded almost immediately. They messaged back and forth a few times and finally set up a meeting place and time.

A spark ignited at that meeting, and their passion for each other silenced their convictions. King David, the human described as a man after God's own heart, is now an adulterer.

Bathsheba sneaked back into her house, and a few weeks later, David received a text from her saying she was pregnant. Both were freaked out. Bathsheba assumed she was unable to have children. She and Uriah had been married for years and had never conceived. David tried to calm her while plotting a way to cover up the affair.

He came up with Plan A. If he could get Uriah home to spend a weekend with his wife, no one would know it wasn't Uriah's baby.

David emailed General Joab, telling him that he had approved a weekend pass for Uriah and to please send him home.

Confused, Uriah returned to Jerusalem and reported to the king's office. After inquiring about the battle, David instructed Uriah to spend the next few days with his wife. But Uriah refused. He felt too guilty. Israel was at war, and his friends were pulling double shifts to cover his duty. He begged to go back to his troops. David encouraged him to stay.

During the next two days, David tried everything to get Uriah to go home, but he refused. Uriah laid out the bedroll he carried on his back and slept outside the palace each night.

David then resorted to Plan B. He planned Uriah's death. Stage the murder to look like another war casualty, and then David would marry Bathsheba.

He tried to contact General Joab, but the officer's phone went to voicemail. The army moved to a location where internet service was nonexistent, so the king handwrote the note, and Uriah returned to battle armed with weapons, supplies, and a letter containing the details of his death sentence.

General Joab followed the orders, placing Uriah on the front lines of the battle. Joab ordered everyone not on the front line to draw back as the fighting intensified. Uriah, along with several other soldiers, was killed almost immediately.

King David was now a murderer.

Bathsheba received he news of her husband's death. She was also notified that the government would cover all funeral expenses. Within weeks of the funeral and before her pregnancy is evident, King David proposes. During a small, informal ceremony, they were married by the Justice of the Peace.

Nine months later, their son arrived, and their pastor, Reverend Nathan, came for a visit. David welcomed him in, thinking he was coming to congratulate the couple and possibly bless the new baby.

After exchanging pleasantries, Pastor Nathan began telling David a terrible story. In his tale, a wealthy man had unexpected company at his house. Instead of cooking meat out of his freezer, he sneaked into his neighbor's house, stole his last roast, and prepared it for his guests.

David was furious and demanded "Tell me his name! I will ensure he is punished to the fullest extent of the law!"

Pastor Nathan's steady gaze bored through David as he announced, "You are the man!"

David's fury instantly turned to sorrow and repentance. His pastor informed him that although God had forgiven him, there were consequences to his actions.

Within a few days, the baby became ill. Before they had an opportunity to come up with a name, the baby died.

After his death, David prays what is now Psalm 51:10. Before we go to verse 10, I want to introduce verses 1–4.

"Have mercy upon me, O God, according to your lovingkindness; According to the multitude of your tender mercies, blot out my transgressions. Wash me thoroughly from my iniquity and cleanse me from my sin. For I acknowledge my transgressions, and my sin is ever before me" (NKJV).

I don't know the exact day I noticed my scars for the first time. But, once I saw them, I couldn't un-see them.

As I wrote before, these weren't ordinary scars. Just like King David's horrific sins, my scars were thick and protruding. Some were as thick as my little finger. They pulled at the skin around them, making simple things like closing my mouth and turning my head difficult.

Every time I entered the office of my plastic surgeon, I wanted to know, "What is your plan to get rid of my scars?"

They consumed my thoughts, and they defined me. Just as King David's sins, my scars were ever before me.

My emotional scars were more extensive than the physical ones on my neck. Between believing I was physically unattractive and the abuse from my father, my self-esteem was almost nonexistent.

I often transferred my feelings of inferiority onto other people. If someone looked at me funny, it was because of my scars. If they were rude to me, it was because of my scars. If they were nice to me, it was because they pitied me because of my scars.

The girl in this picture was miserable. I had not brushed my hair that morning. I had no reason to smile. If I felt anything, it was shame. The girl in my senior picture had been sexually abused more than once.

Earlier chapters included stories of my father's abuse. But when I was in my thirties, I learned that both of my parents had also had long-term affairs.

My parents were my pastors. And those spirits attracted similar spirits. Our church was filled with sexual predators and immoral people. By the time we reached junior high, all five of us (myself and my four sisters) had been sexually abused by people in our church.

My parents knew about some of them, but nothing was done. Nothing.

My nighttime prayers were similar to David's: "Blot out my scars. Make them disappear. They are all I see every day."

The recorder in my head constantly repeated every negative word spoken over me. I was a failure. I knew I was a failure. And for years, no one's voice overrode that of my father.

I made sure I reminded myself of his words every day. I cried about it. I held pity parties for myself, and no one was invited.

With each new offense, the emotional scars grew thicker. Focusing on them gave me an excuse to behave terribly and not be productive in the kingdom of God. Just like the scars on my neck restricted my movement, the scars on my heart kept me stuck in a prison of misery.

Back to the Bible story: David could have stopped with this prayer. After all, it was a sincere prayer of repentance. He took ownership of his sin. He knew he was guilty. He even expected punishment.

I believe David was called "a man after God's own heart" because he chose not to stop there.

If we skip to verse 7 (NKJV), we see David's prayer continue, "Purge me with hyssop and I shall be clean; Wash me and I will be whiter than snow."

That sounds a lot like preparation for surgery. When I was old enough to bathe myself, I was told to wash with a particular soup that would remove germs and bacteria before every surgery. When I was transferred to the surgery table, more products were applied to the area of my body affected by the procedure. The surgeon needed me to be as clean as possible before he would make the first incision.

In verse 10 of Psalm 51, David gets brave and prays, "Create in me a clean heart, O God, and renew a right spirit within me."

That's reconstructive surgery! David permitted God to perform reconstructive surgery on his heart because he took ownership of the condition of it. He recognized that he had an impure heart and a wrong spirit. A reconstructive surgery by the Master Physician changed the way he talked.

When I was eighteen, I began seeing a new plastic surgeon named James Dowd. He seemed to understand exactly how I viewed myself and began outlining steps that would be taken to improve my looks and self-image.

I agreed to every idea Dr. Dowd suggested. He wanted to try radiation to soften and reduce the scars. He cautioned that infertility was a possible side effect.

I asked, "Where do I sign?"

The treatments did not affect the scar tissue at all.

He had also noticed that I did not have bottom teeth in the front. As I said earlier, they had created a chin from a rib, but no gum was in the front. Therefore, there were no teeth.

Dr. Dowd scheduled his first reconstructive surgery on me. He was so eager to help me that he may have done too much. My body instantly began fighting the changes. I ended up in the intensive care unit semiconscious. When I became aware of my surroundings, I discovered I lay in a bed of ice. The nurses were trying to lower my temperature.

When I was fully awake, Dr. Dowd was notified. He began apologizing before he reached my bedside. At this point, I realized that he hadn't just crafted a gumline for me; in his attempt to prevent my tongue from adhering to the healing wound, he had stitched it to the side of my mouth.

I couldn't speak. I couldn't move around. My eyesight was too poor to be able to see the television. I was miserable. I insisted on having a pen and paper so I could write.

My first question was, "When can I see my mom?"

I was told she would be allowed in during visiting hours and when the next one was.

I wrote, "What time is it now?"

I must have asked that question too many times because the nurses moved my bed to a place where I could see the clock and the door visitors came through. I still remember seeing my mom's face pressed against the glass, waiting for the doors to open.

As soon as the gumline healed, a dental appointment was made, and molds were done on my teeth. At nineteen, I received my first bridge and had bottom teeth in the front. It changed how I talked!

We see the change in David's speech in Psalm 51:14–15 (NKJV): "...my tongue shall sing aloud of your righteousness...and my mouth shall show forth your praise."

In the remainder of the psalm, David says things like, "Then, I will teach transgressors your ways, and sinners shall be converted...

"My tongue shall sing aloud of your righteousness.

"My mouth shall show forth your praise."

Mentally, I had to change my speech and my thought process. There could be no internal healing without it.

Let me explain a little. 1 Corinthians 13 is often referred to as the love chapter. I've heard it referenced in weddings and vow renewals. It is also the recipe for healthy Christian living.

Now, you can go back and read through the entire chapter, but I found the layout of it compelling. And just like with David's story in 2 Samuel, I rewrote it.

This is the PKLV: Paul begins by telling us off. He says that even though we can speak several languages, speak in tongues, prophecy, have faith that moves mountains, give everything we own to those in need, and sacrifice our lives to the point of becoming a martyr, it means nothing if we don't have love.

Then, he tells us what love is. It is patient and kind, doesn't envy, and isn't prideful. After that, he launches into the hard part. Love does not behave indecently, is not demanding, is not easily provoked, and neither is it destructive.

Love does not normalize poor behavior but celebrates personal excellence. It also protects important relationships when something threatens to destroy them. It trusts Jesus to help work things out.

Lastly, love holds fast to faith, principles, and priorities until the storms are over.

As I finished writing these verses in my version, I thought, "And just how are we supposed to do that, Paul?"

Paul must have known I would ask that question because, in verse 11, he gives us instructions on how to accomplish this feat. "When I was a child, I spake as a child, I understood as a child, I thought as a child: but when I became a man, I put away childish things" (NKJV).

What were the childish things? What I said, what I understood, and what I thought.

Paul says first, we must change what we say. Why would this be the first step? I think it's because we believe in the voice we hear the most. And sadly, my voice was screaming at me, drowning out everything else.

Yes, my dad's words were loud. But I repeated them in a deafening volume.

Once I began to say the right things, my understanding began to change, and my thought process began to mature. In other words, I grew up.

I became my own "Edna Mode" in my favorite movie, *The Incredibles*, and looked at myself in the mirror, slapped my face, and said, "Pull yourself together!"

Over the next two years, Dr. Dowd tried several procedures to reduce the size of my scars. But they were stubborn and refused to lie flat.

During a monthly checkup, I pleaded with him to find another way to reconstruct my neck. He claimed to have exhausted his options but promised to continue to look for others.

The following week, he called me into his office and laid out a new plan. He was going to try a procedure that, up to this point, had only been used on burn victims.

He would insert balloons under the skin of my neck, and every week, I would go in so he could inject saline into those balloons. The stretched balloons, in turn, would stretch my skin. He explained, "If I can stretch your skin enough to cover the gap made when I cut out the old scars, the new scars will be thinner and lie flatter."

When the time came to remove the balloons, I knew it would probably be my last surgery. I begged, pleaded, and argued until I convinced my surgeon to allow me to stay awake during the procedure.

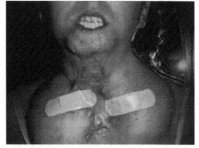

I wanted him to "create in me" a new scar, but I wanted to watch him do it.

Reluctantly, he agreed only to use a mild sedative and local anesthesia. The surgical team would have a mirror set up so that I could watch.

On the day of the surgery, I was wheeled into the operating room and greeted like a celebrity. It was exciting. Everyone was bustling around, preparing for the procedure. Knowing I was awake, they included me in the conversations and explained their part in the grand event.

The surgery began. Not long after the first cut, I felt the pain. I quickly let Dr. Dowd know, and he stopped everything to administer more local anesthesia. The team chatted among themselves as they waited for the drug to take effect.

I stopped him several more times during the next hour. I could feel the knife. The cuts were painful. Patiently, he would stop and administer more anesthesia before continuing.

I finally permitted him to put me to sleep.

When I woke up, I viewed what I believed was the most beautiful scar in the world! It lay flat. The stitching was perfect. The surgeon made sure no detail was forgotten.

My bottom lip had always had a dip where the scar on my chin intersected with it. Dr. Dowd had fixed it, giving me an even bottom lip. He removed a couple of moles from my face and neck without me asking.

I was elated.

As I mulled over the events of that surgery, considering Psalm 51:10, I thought, "How many times have I prayed a 'Create in Me' prayer and stopped God in the process because I decided it was too painful for me to bear?

When I got serious about praying Psalm 51:10 over my life, the Master Physician began to stretch me.

God called me to public speaking.

The level of emotional discomfort with this assignment was off the charts. I reminded God that I looked weird and sounded funny. Also, I was terrified to get up in front of anyone. He acted like He didn't hear my excuse. He began to open doors for me to speak at high schools, businesses, civic organizations, churches, and marriage seminars. In 2021, I delivered a speech standing on the steps of our Louisiana State Capital building.

All these speaking engagements were by invitation. God wasn't playing.

———

As a child, I became a people pleaser because I thought it was the only way people would like me. As I matured, that desire to please people became a messianic or messiah complex. I had to look up the term because I knew what I was doing had to have a name.

People with a messianic complex believe they are responsible for saving or assisting others. I spent hours trying to save people who didn't want to be saved.

When I complained and cried out to God to reconstruct my life, He began cutting away toxic relationships I had created. I would beg Him to stop and instead just put a Band-Aid on the cut. It was a chaotic cycle of releasing control to God and taking it back. Before long, if I was in charge, my life began to spiral out of control again.

When I tried to control uncontrollable people, I lost control of myself.

I finally succumbed to the anesthesia and allowed God to perform the surgery. It was painful. During the process, the pain became so intense that I ended up in counseling. But I'm proud to tell you that the surgery was a success!

When God began stretching me by using us to speak at marriage conferences, I was consuming books on relationships. Without realizing it, He began healing those scars inside of me. Gradually, the bitterness and hatred I had been harboring since I was a child began melting away. The new "scar" was smooth and barely noticeable.

If you return with me for a minute to King David's story, I'll wrap up this chapter.

The story began with King David staying home and sending people to fight his battle. This is a warning for all of us: every time we allow someone else to fight our battles, we are defenseless against temptation.

The battle was against the city of Rabbah. That was the place where David had Uriah killed.

Nine months later, the baby was born and died, and the Israelite army was still at the same place fighting the same battle.

General Joab sends an email to King David stating, "I've been fighting your battle and seized their water supply. But if you want the victory, you'd better gather some men and get over here to help us surround the city. Or else, the victory will have my name on it" (2 Samuel 12:26–28 PKLV).

In 2 Samuel 12:29, David gathered the rest of his army and won the battle of Rabbah.

I looked up the name "Rabbah" and found that it means "abundance or increase; to be more; to become great."

The life I have now is nothing like the one I started with. The chaotic home life I grew up in is not one my children have ever experienced. "Great" and "abundant" are better descriptions of the life I now live.

God did His part, but for me to claim victory, there were facts I had to face and conquer on my own. Praying "create in me a clean heart and renew within me a right spirit" works! For years, all I was good at was creating a filthy heart and renewing a wrong spirit. It's still a daily decision not to return to those old thought processes.

But I've found, just as it was with King David, it doesn't matter how royally we mess things up; if we allow the Creator to perform reconstructive surgery in our lives, He enables us to fight our battles confidently and obtain victory.

I don't remember the last time I noticed the scars. The physical ones or the emotional ones. The Master Surgeon cut out the scar tissue I had allowed to build up. Then, He "gave me a new heart and put a new spirit within me. He took [cut out] my heart of stone. That heart was coated with anger, guilt, jealousy, and bitterness. And He gave [created] a heart of flesh" (Ezekiel 36:26 PKLV).

5

FACING THE FEARS

Fear is temporary. Regret is forever.

He shall cover you with His feathers,
And under His wings you shall take refuge;
His truth shall be your shield and buckler
(Psalm 91:4 NKJV)

In 1999, my mother-in-law, Carol Ann, moved to Jennings. Her trailer was located just minutes from our house. Despite health issues, she was a phenomenal grandmother to my two girls. In late August of 2001, Carol Ann was diagnosed with stage four lung cancer. We were devastated by the news.

Within a week of her diagnosis, Carol Ann was moved from our local hospital to Lafayette General in Lafayette, Louisiana. Our days became a routine of running back and forth from Jennings to Lafayette, keeping up with her steady decline. We prayed for the best but began preparing for the worst.

On September 11, we received a phone call from her doctor that she would need to be placed on a ventilator. The girls were sitting at the breakfast table, and although they didn't understand the gravity of the phone call, their hushed chatter told me they sensed the urgency. Clifton kissed them on the tops of their neatly combed hair and rushed out the door. The procedure would be delayed until he could speak with her, fearing it could be for the last time. Instead of taking his truck, he hopped on his motorcycle, anxious for a brief mental escape on the ride between the house and the hospital.

After dropping them off at school, I returned home to straighten the house and pray. The local Christian radio station kept me company as I moved from room to room.

The emergency alert on the radio sounded, and I dismissed it, believing it was only a test of the Emergency Broadcast System. When the alert sounded a second time, I was closer to the speaker and listened in horror as the announcer began describing the devastation at the Twin Towers in New York City.

My mother-in-law was dying, the United States was under attack, my girls were at school, and Clifton was on his motorcycle, oblivious to the news as well as my repeated phone calls. This was a fear I would have to deal with by myself for a few minutes.

I dropped to my knees in the living room, screaming silently in case anyone walking on the sidewalk bordering the two sides of our corner lot thought Clifton and I were in a domestic dispute. My world was out of control, and there was not one thing I could do about it. I spent several minutes vomiting my fears to a God I couldn't see but needed to trust. My Bible sat on the shelves in the living room, and I reached for it like a drowning person would a life raft.

I turned to Psalm 91 and made it personal (v. 1–2): "You said that he that dwelleth in the secret place of the most High shall abide under Your shadow, Almighty God. I'm claiming that You are **my** refuge and **my** fortress: you are **my** God; in You I trust. (v. 15–16) I will call upon You, and You will answer **me**; You will be with **me** in trouble; You will deliver **me** and honor **me**. With long life, You will satisfy **me** and show **me** Your salvation."

For a moment, I escaped in His presence. The ringing of my cell phone startled me back to reality. It was Clifton, responding to the fifteen missed phone calls from me. I quickly filled him in on this unmitigated act of terrorism happening in our country as he rushed past waiting areas where people huddled in disbelief, their eyes glued to the televisions. Once he arrived in his mother's private room, he could see the devastation on the news. He described the horrific scenes on the screen as we absorbed this horrifying reality.

Our phone call was interrupted by a call from the school. The teachers and administration were struggling with their emotions. Teaching was out of the question. As a result, schools were allowing children to return to the safety of their homes. Nine-year-old Eden and six-year-old Eryn were tearful when they saw my face in the car line. I hadn't thought about how this would affect my girls.

Our house had an upstairs bedroom and bath we used as an office, movie hangout, or guest space. Knowing they needed a distraction, I suggested movie time, and both vehemently shook their heads. An airplane could reach them up there, they fearfully reasoned. It was months before either of them ventured up the stairs.

The next three months were a blur as we kept up with the chaos of 9-11, the decline of my mother-in-law's health, school, home, and church. Our close friends, Jeff and Tami Harpole, checked in with us almost daily. During one of the phone calls, they invited our family to spend Christmas week with their family in Illinois. We knew that Carol Ann would be in the hospital through the holidays, and her siblings were camped out in her room, so we took them up on their offer.

We drove through the night, arriving at dawn the following day. Light snow was falling, and we stood for several moments, soaking up the delightful feeling of soft kisses on our cheeks. The warmth of the greeting from Mom and Pop Harpole (Bill and Rosalee), Jeff and Tami, and Jeff's sister, Dana, made us feel as though we were embracing family. And for the next week, we were treated as such. They even had stockings hanging on the fireplace for each of us. Their thoughtfulness was like a balm to our souls.

The week of celebrations included cooking, washing dishes, shopping, taking turns in the bathroom, and lots and lots of laughter. Evenings were spent in the living room, visiting and enjoying the warmth of the fireplace. I don't remember everything we said, but I remember how I felt as I watched Mom and Pop Harpole interact with their grown children. It was what I wanted for my life. I had never seen adults be together for this long without screaming and fighting.

I experienced a godly, healthy, happy home for a solid week. I left with a mission to create that atmosphere for my children. It was my responsibility to be the cycle-breaker.

———

The twenty-fifth chapter of Matthew talks about responsibilities. Well, it actually speaks of talents. A talent is a condensed description of many things, such as money, gifts, and weights.

I'm taking a bit of literary license here and replacing the word "talent" with the word "responsibility."

Matthew 25:14–15 says, "For the kingdom of heaven is like a man traveling to a far country, who called his own servants and delivered his goods to them.

"And to one he gave five responsibilities, to another two, and to another, one, to each according to his own ability; and immediately he went on a journey."

The Scriptures don't say whether or not instructions were given or if expectations were clearly explained. It says, "Immediately after handing out responsibilities, he left on a journey."

The story continues in the following verses and lets us know that the servant who was given five responsibilities mastered them and added an additional five. The servant with two responsibilities ended up with four. But the one handed only one responsibility decided to dig in the earth and bury it.

For the following few paragraphs, I want to tell you about that person who buried his responsibility. I know him well. But actually, he is she, and for much of my life, I did my best to keep the responsibility of breaking a cycle buried.

I thought I had a good excuse. I was born defective and belonged to a dysfunctional family. As long as I wasn't as bad as they were, I patted myself on the back, believing I was doing my best.

My weaknesses were glaring, but my low self-image caused me to believe that any attempt to change would be disappointing. Where would I even begin?

I was married to the prince I wrote about in my children's book, *The Perfectly Imperfect Princess: An Unfairy Tale Gone Right*. But unlike the Disney fairy tale endings (which is how I ended my book), we did not live happily ever after. I packed up the chaos from my childhood home and brought it and over a hundred pairs of shoes into our marriage.

Not only was I a hot mess when we got married, I was still struggling with my thoughts and behavior after I had children. I knew I had a responsibility, and generations would be positively affected if I answered the call.

As much as it hurt, I dug it up, faced my fears, and began to work on them. I read books, went to counseling, and made myself accountable. Breaking toxic cycles was not easy. I knew how to behave in public. It was in private that my actions needed work. My husband and daughters were witness to my overreacting and narcissism.

I learned it was much easier to do the right thing than to think the right thing.

—————

I was a Spirit-filled Christian, but like my father, any fruit of the Spirit developed in me was carefully packaged and served to people who didn't matter. I realized that if I were going to break the cycle, I would serve that "fruit" at home first.

If you want to know who I really am, don't ask the people who attend our church or those who see me in the community. Ask my husband, daughters, or sons-in-law. Their opinion is the one that matters.

If we go back to our parable in Matthew 25 (and I will paraphrase), it tells us that after a long time, the lord of those servants came and settled accounts with them.

The one with five responsibilities came and brought a list of five more responsibilities he had completed. The one with two responsibilities with two responsibilities came and brought proof of two more.

Then, the one with only one responsibility dug it up and delivered it to his lord. But instead of presenting a list of more accomplishments, he brought a list of excuses: he was a victim and afraid. His refusal to face his fears rendered him helpless.

We would have felt sorry for him.

The Scripture says the lord called him "wicked" and "lazy" and handed that servant's responsibility over to the one who had ten.

Had I not dug up my responsibility and changed my thoughts and behavior, some licensed counselors who had doubled their responsibilities would have been given the responsibility to help my daughters. If I had not changed, my sons-in-law would have borne the weight of my daughters' mental healing.

Before I end this chapter, I want to share five things I learned from this story:

1. Not everyone has the same gifts and talents, but everyone has a responsibility.

2. There is no mention of retirement in this story. In fact, the servants who doubled their responsibilities were promised even greater responsibility.

3. The responsibility given to the wicked servant was a necessary one. The master didn't just dismiss the task because the servant was unwilling to fulfill it.

4. Everyone is capable of fulfilling their responsibility. The Scripture clearly states that each servant was handed the responsibilities according to their ability.

5. I am proof that as long as you are breathing, it is possible to change from being a wicked servant to a good and faithful one.

In the words of Leo Buscaglia,

"Your talents (responsibilities) are God's gift to you; what you do with them is your gift back to God."

6

FACING THE FUTURE

Defining moments aren't always planned, or appreciated,
until you look in the rearview mirror.

The surgery to create a chin was a turning point in my development. In all of the pictures taken before this surgery, my mouth hung open. After the healing process was complete, I now could shut my mouth. The new "chin" also enabled me to speak clearly. But it would be years before I would learn what I needed to say.

After watching the movie *War Room*, I created a prayer closet in one of my guest bedrooms. In that closet, I taped inspirational Scriptures that resonated with me all over the wall. Those Scriptures are my lifeline during various storms. My prayer closet is a place of refuge I run to every morning and sometimes throughout the day.

One such morning, as I sat quietly reading the Scriptures on the wall, one stood out, and God began to speak to me as I read it.

Mark 11:22–24 (NKJV) says, "So Jesus answered and said to them, 'Have faith in God. For assuredly, I say to you, whoever says to this mountain, "Be removed and cast into the sea", and does not doubt in his heart, but believes that those things he says will be done, he will have whatever he says. Therefore I say to you, whatever things you ask when you pray, believe that you receive them, and you will have them.'"

As I stared at the Scripture in silence, God spoke these words: *"Most of your mountains are in your mind. I've fully equipped you to conquer those mountains, but you tend to avoid them and accept defeat."*

Dr. Caroline Leaf is a neuroscientist who has studied mental health for years and is an expert on the mind. She says every thought becomes a substance (plantlike image) in our brain. Good thoughts blossom and look like healthy trees. Bad thoughts look like scrawny, sickly trees. Dr. Leaf teaches that we can change our brains by controlling our thoughts. Our thoughts cannot control us. They merely affect us. (Leaf, 21-Day Brain Detox 2019)

In Hebrews 11:1 (NKJV), Scripture backs that up when it says, "Now faith is the *substance* of things hoped for, the *evidence* of things not seen."

Faith is a mental activity. It is believing for something that currently does not exist. Thinking and speaking faith becomes a SUBSTANCE in our brain. *Faith is a substance.* A healthy thought can create a healthy tree in our brains.

If you continue reading Hebrews, in the eleventh chapter, you will see references to biblical heroes who bravely accomplish unbelievable things simply by faith. Verse 8 (NIV) says, "By faith, Abraham, when called to go to a place he would later receive as his inheritance, obeyed and went, even though he did not know where he was going."

I can picture Abraham talking to himself every morning as he packed his duffel bag and encouraged his family to follow him. He didn't know where he was headed but trusted that God was leading him. If Sarah was anything like me, her nagging voice was hammering him: "Do you know where you are going? Are we lost? Why are we moving? Where we were living was great. We were with family. Are you sure God told you to move, or was that indigestion?"

Abraham had to make the voice in his head override the voice of his wife. He may have had doubts, but his faith in God made him continue the journey toward the new land God had picked for him.

Verse 11 says, "And by faith even Sarah, who was past childbearing age, was enabled to bear children because she considered him faithful who had made the promise" (NIV).

Sarah was ninety years old. She was probably in shock when she overheard the angels talking to Abraham and telling him she would have a son. Although she laughed to herself, the Lord heard her, and the angel asked Abraham, "Why did Sarah laugh, saying 'Shall I surely bear a child, since I am old?' Is anything too hard for the Lord?" (Genesis 18:13–14 ESV)

I'm sure Sarah had to talk to herself during those nine months of pregnancy and the delivery process. Can you imagine raising a toddler in your nineties? *Come on, Sarah, you can do this. Just breathe.* We know she was giving herself a pep talk.

Whatever she said to herself gave her the strength she needed to raise the promised child.

Verse 23 says, "By faith Moses' parents hid him for three months after he was born, because they saw he was no ordinary child, and they were not afraid of the king's edict."

This story always gets me. Moses' parents had to be the bravest souls on the planet. Fearful that the numerous Israelites would gain control in Egypt, Pharoah instructed all the Hebrew male children to be thrown into the river. But Moses' parents refused as long as they could.

To save his life, they put him in a basket and sent him floating down the river. I cannot imagine what words his mother told herself to make her fingers uncurl from the edge of the basket.

I'm a mother. How do you place your three-month-old child in a basket and watch it float down a river without screaming in agony? How do you make yourself let go? The Bible tells us how. It was *by faith.* She had to replace her fearful thoughts with faithful thoughts: *He will be okay. He will not die. God has a plan for his life.*

God honored her faith. Not only did Moses not die, but years later, God chose him to lead the children of Israel out of Egypt.

Hebrews 11:30 says, "By faith the walls of Jericho fell after they were encircled for seven days."

If we read the story in the Old Testament, we see that the children of Israel marched around the city without speaking a word. I'm sure they had a lot of questions, but they didn't voice their concerns out loud.

At some point in their wilderness journey, they learned the power of their words. They had witnessed some of their kinfolk perishing at the hand of God for speaking against God's ability to deliver them. They saw the consequences when others spoke against the God-appointed leaders. Even though they could not comprehend how God would give them this walled city just by walking around it, none of them broke the silence.

Daily, they marched, convincing themselves mentally that the walls could fall. And *by faith*, they marched for seven days. On the seventh day, they marched around the city seven times. As they took the final step on that seventh round, they were released to unleash their tongues. The roar shook the heavens and the earth, and the wall between them and their promise crumbled.

Verse 31 of Hebrews 11 says, "By faith the harlot Rahab did not perish with those who did not believe, when she had received the spies with peace."

Rahab was a citizen of Jericho and had aided the Israelite spies. In exchange, they promised that she and her household would be spared. Somehow, even though her reputation was smeared, she convinced her entire family to gather inside her house. The spies had told her that only those *in the house* would be saved.

Joshua 2:15 lets us know that Rahab lived on the city wall. She had a front-row seat to the army of Israelites circling the city. Can you imagine the faith it took not to run out the door when the wall started falling? Rahab had to have spoken to her fear when it looked like her house was falling apart.

Have you ever been there? Where everything looks hopeless? And nothing was changing, except for getting worse? And all you had to hold on to was a promise?

These people mentioned in Hebrews 11 didn't merely "believe" in their hearts. They confronted their fear of the unknown and spoke aloud the promises God gave them. We have to do the same. Romans 10:17 says, "Faith comes by hearing."

We believe the voice that we hear. Unfortunately, the voice that we hear the most is our own. So, it is up to us to speak to our mental mountains so that they are moved.

Are you like these faith heroes in Hebrews 11? Or are you more like the ten spies in Numbers 13? That chapter tells us that twelve spies were sent to spy out the land God had already promised to give them. It was a done deal. All they needed to do was go and look at it and bring back a report. But once they got there, two spies kept their faith in God, while ten came back to report that victory was impossible.

Numbers 13:32–33 says, "They gave a bad report of the land, saying, 'The land through which we have gone as spies is a land that DEVOURS its inhabitants, and all the people whom we saw in it are men of great stature. There we saw giants (the descendants of Anak came from the giants): and we were like grasshoppers in our own sight, and so we were in their sight.'"

Now, the people of the land did not view the Israelites as grasshoppers. How do I know? I know because, in the book of Joshua, the second chapter, Rahab tells the spies, "I know that the Lord has given you the land...the terror of you has fallen on us, and all the inhabitants of the land are faint-hearted because of you."

What happened between the time they were sent into the land, excited about their future, and when they exited defeated? Answer: they let their insecurities build a monument in their brains. They decided they looked like grasshoppers and projected their thoughts on the people of the land.

But Rahab said, "Our people have *no more courage*...because of you, for the Lord your God, He is God in Heaven above and on earth beneath."

Rahab had more faith in their God than they did.

———

Because I was called "stupid" by my father for years, I lacked confidence as an adult. Believing I was not intelligent became a mental mountain.

James 1:5: "If any of you lacks wisdom, let him ask of God, who gives to ALL liberally and without reproach, and it *will be given* to him."

Repeatedly, I asked for wisdom. I spoke that verse over my situation. As God gave me direction, I added Proverbs 3:5–6 to my memory instead of questioning it.

"Trust in the Lord with all your heart. And lean not on your own understanding: In all your ways acknowledge Him, and He shall direct your paths" (NKJV).

I've learned that you automatically get smarter when you go to God for direction. His Spirit will lead and guide you into better decisions for your life.

2 Timothy 1:7 says, "For God has not given us a spirit of fear, but of power and of love and of a sound mind" (NKJV).

A sound mind.

A rational mind.

This is one of my favorite Scriptures. It has helped me move so many mental mountains.

One of those mountains was the fear of flying alone. I had flown numerous times, but Clifton always accompanied me. I'm unsure if it was a fear of flying or that I wasn't important enough to God for Him to keep the plane in the air. I believed Cliff was more valuable than I to God's kingdom, and therefore, if he were on the flight, it would land safely.

In August of 2010, Clifton was scheduled to speak at a camp meeting in Pennsylvania, and my older daughter, Eden, was starting her first year of college. Not wanting to miss out on either of these events, I decided to stay home with Eden, witness her first couple days of school, and then fly out to meet Clifton for the remainder of the week. For the first time, I would fly alone.

Whenever the fear of flying crept into my mind, I redirected my thoughts. The afternoon before I was to fly out, I was zipping around town running last-minute errands, and without warning, it hit me. Hard. In just a few short hours, I would be on an airplane. All. By. Myself.

The fear that gripped me was tangible. Although the cold air from the car vents was directed toward me, streams of sweat ran down my body, soaking my thin summer dress. I gripped the steering wheel tighter, endeavoring to steady my shaking hands. My breathing sounded like a woman in labor, and my attempts to control it proved futile.

I drove home as fast as I could and ran to my bedroom. No one was at home, so I lay face-down on the carpet and began pleading and begging God to remove the fear from me in the next few minutes. Yes. I gave Him a time limit. I knew my daughters would be home soon, and I could not carry on like a crazy person.

Through broken sobs, I reminded God of His Word. *"Fear is not from you! Please deliver me from it."*

Then, I began to thank Him for answering my request. Within minutes, all fear and anxiety left me. Completely.

By the time Eden and Eryn walked through the door, I was standing at the stove cooking supper, and though they were both sensitive, neither detected the battle that I had fought during their absence.

The next morning, I boarded an airplane, completely confident that God was with me and that there was nothing I needed to fear. I learned later that I had symptoms of an anxiety attack. I've flown multiple times alone since 2010 and have never experienced those feelings.

Philippians 4:6–7 (NKJV) says, "Be anxious for nothing, but in everything by prayer and supplication, with thanksgiving, let your requests be made known to God; and the peace of God, which surpasses all understanding, will guard your hearts and minds through Christ Jesus."

Picture it in your mind. As you are speaking this verse, that Mental Mountain is being moved, and the Mountain of Peace is taking its place.

Regardless of the size of my mountain, it is no match for the Word of God. I learned to speak His Word out loud. The Word works. The Word is alive and creates.

Romans 10:17 says, "Faith comes by hearing, and hearing by the WORD of God."

My voice is the one that I hear the most. I am the one who controls what comes out of my mouth. Therefore, I am the problem, and I am the solution. In order to face the future, I needed to speak Scriptures over my mountains until I was convinced of what I was saying, and I began to see those mountains disappear.

Overcoming the mountains never got easier. I became stronger.

This does not just apply to me. This is a universal principle from the Scriptures. By His Word, God framed the world, so by His Word still creates. He said, "Let there be light," only one time, and we still have light to this day. Personalize and speak the Word into your life, then watch the Word transform you. Be brave. I dare you.

THE ACTION

Christians don't have hang-ups.
They have hang-ons.

Reverend Marty Jeanice

"For behold, I have made you this day a fortified city
And an iron pillar, and bronze walls against
the whole land—
against the kings of Judah, against its princes,
against its priests, and against the people of the land.
They will fight against you,
but they shall not prevail against you.
For I am with you," says the Lord, "to deliver you"

(Jeremiah 1:18–19 NKJV).

7

DEFECTIVE

Mirror, mirror, you're not fair.
You only reveal what's clearly there.
You do not show beneath the skin.
And what lies beneath is where you win.

In the fall of 1968, I met my first human mirror.

It was my first day of kindergarten at the elementary school located in our neighborhood. I walked to school with my oldest sister, Jonette, holding her hand tightly as she filled me in on all the activities she had already experienced.

Jonette had made it to second grade, had her own friends, and could read. She was the smartest, most beautiful girl I knew.

I couldn't wait to meet my classmates, make friends, and begin learning. The anticipation of this new adventure had kept me up most of the night.

Jonette held my hand until we arrived at the door to the kindergarten classroom. She hugged me tightly and promised to wait for me in front of the school at the end of the day. I turned the knob and entered the real world.

Up until this day, I was a celebrity in the medical world and a commoner at home. Doctors and nurses were impressed with my scars as well as my capabilities. Within the walls of our home, I was treated in the same manner as my sisters. Chores, punishments, and presents were distributed evenly.

The teacher welcomed me into the colorful alphabet-decorated classroom, directing me to my seat. My name was neatly written at the top of the paper waiting for me at my desk. That was the only word on the page I could read. I was confident I would be able to read the rest of the words by the end of the day.

Introductions, color pages, and instructions consumed the majority of the morning, and then we were escorted to the playground, where friendships are formed. I smiled at the giggling group of girls walking arm in arm as they headed to the swings. They didn't acknowledge me. I ran toward a trio of boys playing chase, hoping to join in the fun. But no invitation was given.

A lone girl on the slide caught my attention, and I made my way toward her. I recognized her from our classroom and thought maybe she would be my first friend.

By the time I got to her, she had slid to the bottom and was approaching the stairs to ascend again. I waved and smiled timidly and asked if she wanted to play. It was a question I had asked my sisters on multiple occasions. Their response was usually affirmative, and that was my expectation. But she looked at me wide eyed, and instead of answering my question, she had one of her own. "What are all of those lines on your face?"

My smile grew bigger as I explained, "Those are leftover scars from my last surgery. The doctor said they will go away eventually."

She wrinkled her nose, drawing her top lip near it, and her eyes became small slits. I thought she was going to sneeze. Instead, she began her ascent to the top of the slide, tossing the words, "You're ugly. I don't want to play with you," over her shoulder.

I ran to the bathroom as tears welled up in my eyes. I knew exactly what I looked like before I left for school. I checked and double-checked to ensure my hair and my bow were straight. My dress and shoes were new, and I was excited to show them off, but no one had complimented them.

As I stared in the mirror above the sink, my eyes no longer saw the beautiful dress or matching bow. My big brown eyes, decorated with long lashes, and my perfect nose became almost invisible as I scrutinized the scars on my face and neck. They seemed to grow larger the longer I stood there.

I saw myself as that girl did. She was right. I was ugly. A knot formed in my throat and traveled to my stomach. Tears stung my eyes as I viewed a face I needed to accept would always be unacceptable. I didn't need others to feel pity for me. I mastered all I needed for myself by myself.

Self-pity is a self-designed trap.

Self-pity is like placing yourself in solitary confinement while holding the key. It's a self-designed trap.

The rest of that year is still a blur. Although I learned to read, I don't remember having any friends besides my siblings. I wondered if they ever really wanted to play with me or whether they acquiesced because they knew they would be in trouble.

Anytime I looked in the mirror, the scars screamed for my attention. When I looked into people's eyes, I watched for a look of disgust or disdain, reinforcing my belief that they were seeing the same defective face I saw. Seeing myself as I perceived other people saw me became my way of life. I sought approval in every face.

As my self-image diminished, my victim mentality grew. I wanted compliments, but when they were given, I questioned the motive of the giver. Did they mean what they said, or were they feeling sorry for me? If they didn't feel sorry for me, what were they hoping to get from handing out a compliment?

I didn't like me, therefore, no one else could. The person I saw in the mirror was defective and scarred and sentenced to be an outcast. That is until Clifton came along.

We had been close friends for over five years, dating off and on (more off than on). We finally made the decision to date exclusively, which meant that even though we were not engaged, we would not date other people.

We went on weekly dates and had daily phone calls. I would find notes and letters from him under the windshield wipers of my car. Clifton was consistent in telling me how beautiful he thought I was and how he wanted to spend the rest of his life with me.

At first, I didn't believe him. He seemed to be sincere, so I watched him closely to see if he had mental issues. I believed that I was so flawed that only someone who was mentally unstable would consider me beautiful.

He was quick witted, highly intelligent, and spoke with the eloquence of men far beyond his years. Other girls pursued him, so I knew he wasn't settling for someone he didn't want. I allowed his words to sink in, and they began to affect me.

One day, I was talking about him to my mother, and as the words were coming out of my mouth, I realized that he was the first "human mirror" that reflected an image I had longed for everyone to see.

When he asked me to marry him, I didn't have to think about it. He looked past obvious flaws and saw me for who I was. The decision was easy, but changing my thinking was hard. When I wanted to feel sorry for myself, I would point out my flaws to him, and he would declare, "That's not what I see when I look at you."

In the early years of our marriage, I tested his love for me repeatedly. My thinking was actually more defective than my face. Thankfully, he stayed and continued to treat me right when I treated him wrong.

8

DEFENSIVE

"A bad attitude is like a flat tire.
If you don't change it, you won't go anywhere."
Joyce Meyer

I lived in eleven houses before I turned sixteen years old.

One of those moves occurred just after I completed my freshman year of high school. Mom and Dad had a huge fight, and Dad loaded some of his possessions in his utility van and moved out in the middle of the night. We didn't see him for a few days. That was long enough for Mom to find a rented house closer to her job. She moved the six of us into a modest four-bedroom, two-bath home. My sisters and I thought we had died and gone to heaven. We grinned and giggled as we helped Mom pack everything and haul it to our haven. We had begged her to leave him so many times.

After we settled in, Mom sat us down and confided in us that Dad had not been supporting us financially.

She explained that he felt his income from the church was strictly for his needs, and other than paying our house note, he did not provide for us. Mom had spoken with her boss, and he had given her a significant raise so she could take care of us.

A week later, Dad showed up with flowers, a job, and empty promises. Mom caved, and I silently screamed as I helped him carry his belongings into our brief sanctuary.

I hated him. I prayed for him to die more than once. Then I would carry around the guilt of what I was thinking. It was a vicious cycle of torment.

I told Mom he hadn't changed, but she refused to listen.

He proved me right a few days later.

———

A sound and a burn across my legs interrupted my sound sleep. Dad stood over me, swinging his heavy leather work belt, hitting me over and over again. My screams woke the rest of the household.

I didn't have to ask what I had done this time. With every blow, he was yelling something about not having a clean uniform to wear to work that day. His work clothes had to be washed separately, and I was waiting for a full load before washing them. I had already been reprimanded for wasting detergent on a half-empty washing machine. I didn't realize he only had two sets of work clothes.

It was four o'clock in the morning. Tired, hurting, and angry, I got up and completed all of the laundry before leaving for school at 7:10 a.m. I never got behind on laundry again. Never.

———

The summer after I turned seventeen, my parents uprooted us again. We left the nice brick home near the highway and moved to a sad single-wide mobile home in the country. The trailer was brown inside and out and looked like it was tired of having to house anyone. The dirt road and the dirt driveway contributed to a layer of dust inside. I did not want to live there.

Within days of moving in, my dad once again became the warden of our prison. He had us up at 5 a.m. to work outside, building a "garage" for the mobile home. We worked until the temperature became unbearable, and we were allowed to go in, eat breakfast and do chores in the slightly cooler metal oven that was our home.

When Mom came home from work, we helped her cook supper and clean the kitchen. Dad had us working outside again until the sunset. I decided if I ever really went to prison, I would see if I could get credit for time served.

One afternoon during the construction, I was Dad's assistant, handing him nails, hammers, drills, and anything else he needed. He was frustrated, as usual, and I braced myself, waiting for his anger to reach a boiling point.

When he asked me to grab a tool that I had no idea what it was, I broke into a sweat, knowing my lack of knowledge would probably send him over the edge. Desperately praying for an escape route, I searched the work area, hoping it would jump into my hands. It didn't. I turned to ask him to describe it, and I saw the prongs of the extension cord just before it struck me, cutting into the side of my face. I could feel the warm blood mixing with the sweat as it made a path to the collar of my shirt.

A calm rage settled in my slender frame, and I did not utter a sound. This time, I would not give him the satisfaction of knowing he hurt me. In that instance, I made up my mind that he would never see me cry again.

The blood continued to run, and I refused to wipe it. By this time, he had grabbed the tool he needed, and we were working side by side again. I stood where it would be impossible for him not to see the damage he had done to my face. The wound eventually stopped oozing blood, but I left it, allowing it to dry in the summer heat.

The anger became my fuel to stare, emotionless, any time he looked my way. Eventually, he couldn't take it anymore and ordered me to go inside and wash my face before my mom got home.

I became skillful at suppressing my feelings and showing no emotion. It became my superpower.

The statement, "People hide where they're hurting," was something I heard a conference speaker, Vonnie

Lopez, say. Her words resonated so deeply within me that I grabbed my phone and added it to my notes.

What I didn't realize was I would spend the rest of my life working to come out of hiding. Yes, Dad had treated me badly. Yes, I deserved the right to be angry. However, I had allowed the offenses to create a mental and emotional breach, and destructive spirits began to consume my thoughts and behavior.

I sat on a church pew and listened to my dad preach about the goodness of God and the necessity of being a "light" to a dark world, knowing that he wasn't following the principles he taught. Our home did not reflect his message. The duplicity gave me the justification to tune him out. By the time I was eighteen, I could sit straight in church, staring at the preacher, even nodding my head appropriately to what was said, without registering a single word. As soon as the preaching began, I mentally left the building.

Even after Cliff and I became pastors of our church, I realized that I left many church services without hearing one word spoken. In order to break the habit, I began taking notes. Our church thought I was studious, but I wasn't. I was trying hard to pay attention and break a negative mindset. Before it broke me beyond repair.

God could not change my heart if I never allowed Him to speak to it.

Romans 10:14–15;17 (NKJV) says, "How then shall they call on Him in whom they have not believed? And how shall they believe in Him of whom they have not heard? And how shall they hear without a preacher? So then faith comes by hearing, and hearing by the word of God."

My coping skills were not God given. They were learned behaviors due to my circumstances. I taught myself not to forgive. I was convinced that I was a victim, my life was unfair, and therefore, my irrational reaction to negative interactions was justified. Cliff would have to learn to deal with me. It was who I was.

I diagnosed myself with low self-esteem because it shifted the blame for my wrongdoing from me to my dad. It was much easier to blame someone than to work at changing myself.

Before we got married, Clifton sang the hit song by The Police, "Every Little Thing She Does Is Magic." But after we got married and the honeymoon was over, if he offended me in the slightest way, my superpower would kick in, and he would think, *When did she start practicing witchcraft?*

I had not forgiven my father and was making Clifton pay for my dad's sins. To make matters worse, I was repeating my father's rationale: I was punishing Clifton for things he didn't realize he had done wrong.

———

Negativity was my safe space.

Looking back, I also realized that during those years, I didn't have many close friends who weren't related to me. My low self-image caused me to justify putting others down to make myself look good or brag about myself in conversations. I thought I was impressing people. I was wrong. I was pushing people away.

One year, Cliff and I attended a prayer conference in St. Louis, Missouri. Clifton was one of the speakers for the event. After the first night's meeting, we went out to eat and socialize with the other speakers. The restaurant couldn't seat us together, so we split up, females at one table and males at the other.

I had never met any of the women and was intent on making a good impression. The conversation revolved around our children, and I kept interjecting all that I did for my girls. After I'd dominated the conversation for a while, one of the other women stopped me and said, "We know you're the best mother at this table. Now can we talk about someone else?"

I was humiliated and wanted to lash out verbally, but I knew she was right. If I were questioned about the lives of the other people at my table, I would not have had much to say. I was not interested in them, I needed them to be interested in me. I needed their approval in order to feel good about myself.

The other women continued to visit as I stared at my plate until the meal was over. I knew I needed to change but had no clue how to.

As I sat there, God reminded me of the many one-sided conversations I had had with my father. Dad spoke. I listened. Even after I was no longer under his roof.

I'm not sure you can even call them conversations, because he rarely allowed me to speak, except for the one-syllable words that affirmed I was listening.

I would rather cut grass with a pair of scissors than pretend to be interested in his stories about himself. Yet, here I was, repeating the same behavior.

I was determined to change. In the trials God has allowed in my life, I found that when I was negative, the tests were repeated.

—————

My father began talking to Cliff and me about pastoring his church in 1994. Neither of us wanted to be pastors. In fact, God had opened several doors for us to minister in larger churches and conferences. Dreams of traveling and speaking were becoming a reality. We thanked Dad for considering us and refused the offer.

He continued to bring it up and my mom joined his crusade. By December of that year, they were relentless in their efforts to persuade us to accept the position. Both showered us with accolades and reasons why we were perfect for the job. Cliff and I agreed to pray and fast before giving them a final answer.

After much discussion between the two of us, we agreed to assume the pastorate for a period of six months, beginning January 1,1995.

Cliff drew up a document stating Dad's offer, guidelines of the agreement, and it was signed in front of witnesses. One of the guidelines was that my father would not attend during those six months. We believed we would fulfill that short term, resign, and follow our dream of traveling and speaking.

The first Sunday as pastor, Clifton preached, "How to Eat an Elephant." He let the congregation know that we had no clue what we were doing, pastoring was overwhelming, and it was our "elephant." And we would figure it out the same way you eat an elephant, one bite at a time.

Before the end of March, we learned of my father's affair. Apparently, the woman had told her husband about it, and the husband had threatened to make it public knowledge unless my father resigned.

We handled the discovery as discreetly as possible and continued to plow our way through the responsibility of pastoring. The woman and her family moved away and began attending another church.

Cliff and I continued teaching Bible studies as we had before starting to pastor, and new people began attending. Those were "our babies," and we began to feel something we had not felt before—responsibility for the health of the church. Our babies would not survive in an unsanitary environment.

Prayer and fasting contributed to good decisions and as we got closer to the contract deadline, our burden for the church became greater. My father returned for the pastoral election held on the first Sunday of July, and the vote was almost unanimous for us to continue. Only three people cast a "nay."

For better or worse, we accepted the pastorate for an unlimited amount of time. By this time, I was six months pregnant with our second child. Clifton had left his position at the Exxon Refinery in Westlake, Louisiana, and we were living on less than half of the income we were used to. A friend who worked in the state health department learned of our situation and sent me the paperwork to apply for financial help with the medical bills. Within a few weeks, we received a letter confirming that we qualified for government assistance.

Our services were held in a rented building in the center of town that had once housed a lumber/supply store. The property owned by the church had been abandoned for years and was deteriorating. We decided to clean up the debt-free buildings, remodel them, and move back into them.

For the next eight months, we spent evenings and weekends working on the project. Eryn was born on Labor Day weekend and by the time she was two weeks old, I was back at the church doing my part in the process. I remember feeding her, changing her diaper, and rocking her to sleep in that dusty construction zone. After laying her in the portable crib, I would climb scaffolding and paint for a couple of hours until she would wake for another feeding. Eden attended preschool during the morning and her afternoons were spent napping on a pallet on the bare cement floor.

Our first service in the remodeled church was on a Wednesday in March of 1996. Our church was so excited about the move. A fresh coat of paint hung on the interior and exterior of the building. New carpet covered the entire floor. A member of our church had built a custom pulpit and a large curtain hung behind the platform, distracting viewers from the air-conditioning vent positioned just above it. Everything looked shiny, new, and inviting.

My dad attended that service and sat about halfway back on the left side, facing the platform, near the side aisle. We were so proud of the accomplishment and for some reason, thought he would be proud of us too. His face showed no expression as he sat and watched as we sang and worshiped in our "new" facility. Once the preliminaries of the service were over, Clifton began delivering his sermon.

Just minutes into his message, my father stood, walked to the center aisle, and exited the building. My heart hurt as I watched my husband struggle to continue speaking while the congregation became distracted by my father's departure. Once again, he had ruined another celebratory moment. When he was questioned about it later, he claimed he had taken medicine and it made him feel unstable, and he felt it was better to leave than to make people worry about him.

I knew better. He wanted everyone to see he was not supportive of our efforts. If he felt uneasy, the wall would have provided support for his "unstable" body. It wasn't long before he confirmed my suspicions. Church members began reporting that he had been to their home claiming we had stolen the church from him.

They didn't know him like I did. Clifton was not even aware of the level of abuse he had committed. I spent hours defending myself and my husband to people who Dad had poisoned with his tongue. Cliff and I were physically and emotionally drained for the remainder of that year.

Just before November, Dad told us of his plans to go on a mission trip to the Philippines. We were elated. Not only would he have a purpose, but he would be out of the country and our lives for three whole months.

The Sunday before he left, he attended church with us, and Clifton had our congregation pray for him and we took up an offering to help with his expenses. That was the last day of our "normal" life as a family.

The next day, my mom dropped my father off at the airport and, before nightfall, moved in with her boss, a widowed man thirty years older than her. She waited until she knew my dad would not be able to harm her before making the move. We found out later Dad had threatened to kill all of us and then himself if she ever left him.

As pastors, we were still "eating the elephant," but this bite threatened to choke the life out of us. We had no clue how to handle this. My parents were the previous pastors, and our congregation had just worshiped with them the day before. We couldn't be discreet about this. We had spoken with Mom, who was unwilling to cut off her relationship and move back home.

Cliff made a phone call to the superintendent of the state for our organization, and he told us what to do. We would have to get in touch with my father and tell him to return home. I was terrified and begged Cliff not to call him. My mother begged as well, and when he insisted that it was the right thing to do, she said, "I regret ever suggesting that you two would make great pastors. I was wrong."

Clifton got in touch with my father, and within a few days, he returned home. My stomach was in knots as I waited to see how he would react to the situation.

True to his character, Dad did not accept any of the blame for Mom leaving him. He was angry with her, and he was furious with Cliff and me.

A phone call from him a few days after his return sent chills down my spine. In his cold, calculated voice, he described in detail how he would wire my house to spark a fire that would burn it to the ground with us trapped inside. He boasted that no one would ever discover he was the arsonist.

As he rattled off his plot, my superpower kicked in, and in an emotionless voice, I bid him goodbye and hung up the phone. I did not sleep well for days. Nightmares played out images and sounds of our destruction.

I promised myself that he would not get near either of my children. It was an easy promise to keep because he was not interested in getting to know either of them. When they were teenagers, they attended a wedding where he was a guest. They approached him and greeted him with a hug. He had to ask their names.

9

DEFENDER

Two weeks after Dad's departure to the Philippines, my parents were divorced, and Mom was remarried. The whirlwind surrounding those two weeks did not allow for us to process everything. "Drowning above water" would be a perfect description of myself as well as my sisters.

My mom had purchased the accounting office where we both worked. At the time of her divorce, I had been employed for fifteen years. Dad was a frequent visitor during those years, He would seldom stop by my office on his way to my mother's office. He was focused on checking up on her or getting her to handle business for him. His presence was often unsettling, but Mom never stopped him from coming.

After their divorce, Dad began showing up in my office when Mom wasn't there. He wasn't there to visit me. It was to get information about Mom and to attempt to discredit her in my eyes.

I didn't need his help for that. Both had lived deceitful lives and although I honored them because the Bible commands me to, I did not respect either of them.

When he would show up in my office, I would give him a stiff hug, offer him something to drink, and ask how he was doing. He never reciprocated the question. All the conversation was one sided.

I sat and listened as he vented about my mom and how she had ruined his life, bragged about his ministry opportunities, or shared biblical insight that he was positive would transform my life. I had quit taking spiritual advice from him years before.

About six months after their divorce, he walked into my office and began speaking before he sat down. It was clear he had a message he needed to get out of his system, so the "unusual" pleasantries were bypassed.

In hopes of getting rid of him, I told him I had a deadline to meet and would have to continue to work while he talked. Dad didn't like it when you didn't look at him while he was talking. My plan didn't dissuade him. He launched into his usual rant about my mom while I stared at the computer and typed out unintelligible words and sentences, trying to appear hard at work.

I bit my tongue, knowing that anything I said would not be well received and would only incite his anger. The conversation began with him announcing that I was on my mom's side. That was his perception. I wasn't for either of them. I tuned him out as much as I could but occasionally nodded or made a sound to make him believe I was listening.

My ears perked up when I heard him say my husband's name. I stopped pretending to work and stared at him as he began speaking negatively of Clifton. He had convinced himself, and was trying to convince me, that my husband was the root of his problem. He began calling my husband names and claiming Clifton was a liar and a manipulator.

I'm not sure what response he was expecting, but his eyes made it apparent that it was not the one I chose. He had crossed my invisible boundary line.

I stood up and stared into his eyes with as much bravery as I could muster. I knew what he was capable of, and every joint in my body began to dance to a silent, up-tempo beat. If he noticed I was shaking, he didn't comment on it.

Before I lost my confidence, I blurted out,

"You are no longer welcome in this office. I've listened to you complain about your life that is a result of your poor choices and not said a word.

"I've kept my mouth shut while you blamed my mother for your unhappiness and refused to take sides. But I will not be silent while you disrespect my husband.

"You have lied to me. Mom has lied to me. But Clifton has been honest with me since the first day I met him. He has provided the security I lacked from you.

"If you are hoping I will choose sides between you and my husband today, you need to know that you lost. You will never speak negatively to me about Clifton again."

We stared at each other for what seemed like minutes before he turned and walked out the door, slamming it behind him. The sound did not send me into a panic. The cloak of fear was no longer wrapped around my shoulders. It had slipped unnoticed to the floor. The slam of the door was one of victorious finality. I had stood up to my adversary and he fled. He was a bully and only preyed on those he could intimidate.

For the remainder of his life, Dad never spoke negatively about Clifton in my presence. I would hear rumors of what he said about Clifton from other people, but he never crossed that line with me.

Proverbs 18:21 says, "Death and life are in the power of the tongue."

It was difficult not to repeat the actions of my father. His poor choices had consequences and so did mine. Like him, I saw myself as the victim instead of the key to my own success.

The lack of joy in my life was totally dependent on what I was thinking and saying. To distract myself from my own misery, I focused on other people's mistakes and failures. Airing others "dirty laundry" gave me a false sense of superiority. But at the end of the conversation, I felt as dirty as if I had physically handled their soiled undergarments. There was not one time I remember feeling good after talking bad.

No one wants all their secrets exposed for everyone to view, least of all myself. But gossip had become a dirty bandage I used frequently to cover my wounds.

I since learned when I am defending other people's reputations, I am defending and protecting my own.

The children of Israel's thinking was just like mine for most of my life. Highly toxic. Very few of the Israelites had a positive attitude about their situation. In fact, I don't know if there were any optimists among them besides Moses and his brother, Aaron. The Bible says that the *whole congregation* murmured. They had been in survival mode for so long they couldn't get it through their thick skulls that God wanted them to *thrive!*

As soon as they left Egypt and the Egyptians were no longer a threat to them, they stopped and worshiped God. They were free from slavery, and ahead of them was the Promised Land.

But within two months, they ran out of the rations they had brought with them and began to do what they were good at, complaining. By this time, they had traveled far enough away that Egypt did not seem like such a bad place anymore.

Exodus 16:2–3 (KJV) records, "And the *whole congregation* of the children of Israel murmured against Moses and Aaron in the wilderness: And the children of Israel said unto them, 'Would to God we had died by the hand of the Lord in Egypt, when we *sat* by the *flesh [meat] pots*, and when *we did eat bread to the full!* For you brought us forth into this wilderness, to *kill this whole assembly with hunger!*'"

They hadn't been sitting by pots of meat. They had been working and living like slaves. Exodus 1:13–14 tells us that "the Egyptians made the Israelites serve them with rigor [harshness or cruelty]. And they made their lives bitter with hard bondage [labor] in mortar, in brick, and in all manner of service in the field." Verse 23 gave us the reality of what life was like when it said, "Then the children of Israel groaned because of the bondage, and they cried out; and their cry came up to God because of the bondage."

They certainly weren't casually sitting and visiting, pots of meat simmering nearby.

But after they were delivered, after God showed up and showed off getting them out of slavery, they soon complained. And when God heard it, He gave Moses His plan, "Behold, I will rain bread from heaven for you; and the people shall go out and gather a certain rate every day, that I may prove them, whether or not they will walk in my law, or not."

Notice that God said, "I'm going to prove them," meaning "I'm going to test them" by providing manna to see if they would obey Him.

According to the Scriptures, God tested them for the next forty years by providing daily manna. It was *mercy manna*. Each day, God would provide the manna and think, *Maybe today they will trust me and walk in my law.*

And the Israelites built an idol, a golden calf.

Then, the next day, mercy manna would fall, and God would give them another opportunity to walk in His law.

And the Israelites complained about their lack of water.

Mercy manna continued to fall daily, and the congregation continued to turn against the leadership.

Regardless of their behavior after they collected manna, the manna appeared again the next day. The opportunity to live according to their faith presented itself *every day*.

While I've heard this story in Sunday school and in sermons throughout my life, one story never made sense to me: the story recorded in Numbers 11. This is the account of when the children of Israel got tired of manna, complained, and asked for meat, and God got angry.

Why would the request make Him angry? They just wanted a change in the menu. I would have wanted the change as well. There's only so much you can do with manna. And if you're on a keto diet, you can't have it.

As I researched the history, I found another account in Exodus 16. In verse 8, we find Moses telling the people what God had told him: "This shall be, when the Lord shall give you in the evening **flesh to eat,** and in the morning bread to the full."

In verses 13–15, it says, "And it came to pass, that at even [evening] the **quails came up**, and covered the camp; and in the morning when the dew was lifted, there lay a small round thing… And when the children of Israel saw it, they said one to another, 'It is manna.'"

They were receiving meat all along. From the very first day, they received quail in the evening and manna in the morning. So, what was the problem?

I looked up the word "quail" and found that it comes from the Hebrew word "slav." Add an "e" to "slav" and you have the word "SLAVE." It was their "slave mentality" that kept them thinking their past was better than their future.

And isn't that true of us too? Slave mentality always glamorizes our past every time our present becomes uncomfortable.

I also looked up the word "manna." It means "What is it?" Manna was something from heaven that appeared each morning, and they went to sleep each night, trusting God would send exactly the amount needed the next morning.

Numbers 11:4 (NKJV) says, "Now the mixed multitude who were among them yielded to **intense craving;** so the children of Israel also wept again and said, 'Who will give us meat to eat?'"

Another word for "quail" is "flesh." Flesh is carnal or earthly. Manna was "heavenly." The problem wasn't that they didn't have a variety in their diet. The problem was that they had lost their appetite for the things of God. The Bible says, "They were consumed with their lusts."

God was angry because they were consumed with their own fleshly desires. The bottom line, they became carnal.

When I think of the word "carnal," I see "CAR." A "CAR" is a vehicle that gets you from one place to the next. Our "FLESH" is the vehicle that will get us from this earth into eternity. When your "CAR" doesn't want to take you to church, make time to pray, or read His word, there's a strong probability you are CARNAL.

Quail was easy. They were familiar with quail. Manna was something they had not seen before. They had to learn how to use it. Manna had to be collected, processed, and made into something edible. The Israelites wanted an easier fix for their dilemma.

When the Israelites found themselves in the desert with lots of time on their hands, they had forgotten how to daydream. They forgot how to believe God for a better life. Yes, they had left their past behind and were on their way to a land God promised them, but all their thoughts led them back to Egypt.

God had promised them a land "flowing with milk and honey," but their senses were still filled with the smell of leeks and garlic used to season their meat. It was a scent of familiarity. Their negative thoughts of "This is too hard" and "I can't do it" were poisoning their ability to daydream.

Dr. Caroline Leaf is a brilliant and prolific communication pathologist and cognitive neuroscientist. She studies the effect negative and positive thoughts have on the brain. Leaf suggests that this type of toxic thinking can result in mental and physical damage, setting the stage for future mind and brain issues, which are preventable. (Leaf, 21-Day Brain Detox 2019)

Their solution was to go back to Egypt, but that was never an option for God. Their threats to return to Egypt did not stop God from fulfilling His promise of morning manna. The Israelites wanted an easy fix, and God was looking for their trust that He could fulfill what He promised.

Isn't that what we want? An easy fix? I know that's what I prefer. I entered the wilderness on August 13, 1988, my wedding day. I *thought* I was entering the Promised Land. I left behind the abuse and instability of my parents' home. But I carried the negativity into my marriage, making the first fifteen years (or more) the wilderness, with an emphasis on *wild!*

I didn't want to go back to "Egypt" physically, I just mentally escaped there when my expectations weren't met. When I realized how negative my thinking was and began to recognize the damage I was doing to my mind, my body, and my relationships, I went to God.

I thought I was being honest about my faults, but all I was doing was whining and complaining about my situation. I wanted Him to do all the work and let me enjoy the miraculous change.

Just as God provided for the children of Israel in their wilderness, He provides "manna"—something edible from heaven—for each of us. Every morning He tests us to see if we will gather it and trust that it is sufficient for our journey.

I had to develop an appetite for the Word of God to grow and change. The provision was always there, but it was my job to gather the "bread" that would provide nourishment for my mind, body, and soul.

My thoughts should bring a sense of peace. If they don't, I'm "leaning on my own understanding" to work out a situation. I've learned that it is harder to think the right thing than it is to do the right thing.

Whatever situation I faced, there was "manna" for that. I had to look up Scriptures, memorize them, and speak those life-giving words over my situation—a spiritual CPR. This assisted me in approaching the same thing with a different

> It's harder to think the right thing than it is to do the right thing.

perspective. God's perspective. I learned to turn my problems into possibilities for God to intervene on my behalf.

This information would have saved the children of Israel from having to wander in the desert for forty years. I can't judge them. I was nearing my fifties before I became proactive about changing my thought process. The change was made from desperation rather than inspiration. But it was made just in time to handle the storm that was on the horizon.

I remember the day in early February of 2014, sitting in Mom's hospital room while the doctor delivered the news that she had stage four pancreatic cancer. I remember trying to process the news while struggling to breathe beneath the invisible weight that pressed on my chest. I worked hard to keep a brave face on. Mom worked equally as hard. This was an opportunity for God to show up and show off.

The doctor referred us to an oncologist, and the process of fighting cancer began. Immediately, I began searching for manna. The first visit with the oncologist delivered the first bite. On the wall in the waiting area was a sign with Jeremiah 29:11: "For I know the thoughts that I think toward you, saith the Lord, thoughts of peace, and not of evil, to give you an expected end."

We all clung to that verse. It provided nourishment for the moment. Fear did its best to consume our thoughts, but we refused to trade "quail" for "manna." Thoughts of peace gave us strength to endure our wilderness.

I wish I could say that I was brave through it all. There were other things going on in our family, and our church was in the middle of a capital stewardship campaign. I was the interim secretary as well as the accountant for the church. My role as wife and mother did not take a vacation, and it seemed as though I lived from one phone alert to the next.

Every morning, I scrambled around for my "manna." Just one word from God, sent from Heaven, that would nourish my soul for the next twenty-four hours.

Our church had grown beyond our building's capacity, and for the past four years, we had been holding services in a rented facility. To save money to build, we decided to remodel the old building and move back into it until our new building was complete. Any spare moment I had was spent helping with the renovation.

One Saturday morning, I was part of the painting crew. That day, I was exhausted from staying up all night with my mother.

My work was interrupted by a call from my sister, Trudy. Her voice sounded anxious as she asked for prayer for Mom. Trudy was a nurse and had exhausted her efforts but couldn't get the pain under control. Mom's cries in the background made me feel helpless. I was already on my knees trimming the baseboards, so I laid the brush on top of the paint can, bowed my head, and asked God to intervene.

Just moments after I hung up the phone, it rang again. This time it was another family member calling to ask a favor of me. Supposedly I was their last resort, and I angrily washed my paintbrush and jumped in my car to accomplish one more task in my already overloaded day.

Irrational thoughts invited their friends, and they began having a party in my mind. Purely old stupid flesh (carnal) thoughts.

Why do I even try?
Is this the reward I get for serving You, God?
People who don't serve You have it easier than I do!

I was alone in my car on the interstate, and those thoughts became sentences spoken out loud. Before long, I was screaming at the top of my lungs as the torrent of tears erased all signs of makeup. I'm sure any drivers who noticed me that day thought I was crazy, and they wouldn't have been far off. All thoughts led back to quitting. Going back to Egypt. I ended my rant with

WHERE ARE YOU IN ALL OF THIS?
I HOPE YOU'RE GETTING GLORY FROM THIS BECAUSE THAT MAKES ONE OF US!

After my poorly attended pity party ended, the ONE who mattered entered my car. God did not abandon me when I vocalized my fleshly thoughts. He responded with, "I am here. And I am fighting for you."

The tears that streamed were no longer tears of anger. They were tears of determination and resolve. I didn't know how God was going to work it out, but I trusted that He would. Although I felt defenseless against an onslaught of the enemy, I grabbed ahold of my word from Him. My MANNA!

That manna carried me through the next day, which was Sunday, March 9, 2014. After church that morning, I ate lunch with my family, spent time with my mom, caught up on laundry, and did my grocery shopping for the week. By 8:45 p.m., I was bathed and relaxing in bed, and to distract my mind, I began scrolling Facebook. An alert from Facebook Messenger interrupted my perusal, and I tapped to open the message.

It came from a stranger and in a language I couldn't interpret. But I did recognize the last line, "Jeremias 1:18–19". In English, that would be Jeremiah 1:18–19. My first thought was, "Really, God?! You couldn't have sent me a message in my own language?"

I climbed out of bed and looked up that Scripture in my Bible. My manna for the moment read,

"For behold, I have made you this day a fortified city and an iron pilar, and bronze walls against the whole land [then it lists the people in the land]. They will fight against you, but they shall not prevail against you. For I am with you, says the Lord, to deliver you" (NKJV).

That bread from Heaven fed my soul for days as I watched Mom fight for her life.

On May 15, 2014, God answered our prayers, and Mom entered the Promised Land. She was freed from her pain and suffering. She was healed of cancer. It wasn't the way I wanted Him to heal her, but I knew she was healed. As she took her final breath, peace settled over all of us. *He was there.*

There have been many more wilderness experiences since then, but my appetite for manna keeps me on the right track. The daily discipline of gathering manna and applying it to my thought life sustains me.

———

His Word is tried. It is powerful. And it works. Always.

Here's the thing about God's defense. He won't defend those who insist on retaliating or reassigning blame. What do I mean by that? As I unwrapped my actions and began to view them as just that, mine, and began to allow God to dictate when to speak up and when to remain silent, then He began to change my life. God's defense begins on the inside of us. We change, and then our circumstances change.

The deeper we go in seeking His ways and allowing His character to infiltrate our ways, the more absolute His defense.

The name of the LORD is a strong tower;
The righteous run to it and are safe
(Proverbs 18:10 ESV).

CHARACTER DEVELOPMENT

*We don't need self-confidence
we need God-confidence.*

Joyce Meyer

*Therefore, there is now no condemnation for those
who are in Christ Jesus, because through
Christ Jesus the law of the Spirit who gives
Life has set you free from the law of sin and death*

(Romans 8:1–2).

10

LABEL OF SHAME

Shame is a heavy cloak to wear at any age.
It weighed more than I did most of the time.

I spent a lot of time with my paternal grandmother. Her husband, my grandfather, passed away when I was six years old, and she never remarried. I'm not sure if she asked for me to go or if I was dumped on her. I just know I was there a lot.

Maw-Maw Lormand fussed at me often for drooling. I never talked back to her. I loved her fiercely and wanted to please her, but her approval of me was always just out of reach. I slurped and sucked back saliva when I was near her. The sound irritated her, and I got in trouble for that too.

She didn't know I had no feeling in my chin or neck. And I didn't know I was supposed to be able to feel the sensation of the fluids before they ran out of my mouth. To the best of my knowledge, I had not experienced it before.

One day, she looked at me in disgust, pointing to my shirt soaked from the neck to just below my chest. She yanked me by the arm and dragged me to her bedroom, pulling off the shirt while muttering something about hanging a bucket around my neck to collect the saliva. Before she could gain control of her tongue, she referred to me as "Slobber Bucket."

My sisters overheard the term and giggled, "Slobber Bucket." Maw-Maw didn't correct them or apologize. That was my name. I would hear it often until I was in my early teens.

Somewhere amid Maw-Maw's lessons, her tongue got out of control again, and she told me my parents were ashamed to take me anywhere. That's why I stayed with her so much.

To this day, I do not know if it is true. I don't want to know. "Get out of my sight" and "I can't stand the sight of you" were phrases I heard from my father many times. Choking back a sob, I would scurry out of the room like the mice who lived with us. Convinced I was a disgrace, I would hide as much as possible.

Although I haven't heard those phrases in a long time, just writing them down brings back the feeling of shame I felt as a child. I didn't know how terrible these words were until I had children. I've never thought or uttered those words to Eden and Eryn.

Self-esteem is a mental picture we carry around of ourselves. My image was so bad I couldn't bear to look at it either.

11

LESSONS OF SHAME

Saturdays were workdays. I dreaded them. Dad would have projects or yard work for us, and Mom had her list of chores for us as well.

It was a hot August Saturday morning, and my sisters, Jonette and Trudy, and I were picking up toys, sticks, and trash in the yard so Dad could mow. Jonette was ten, I was eight, and Trudy was almost seven. I'm not sure how long we had been working, but I was hot and thirsty, and my bladder was screaming to be emptied.

As I approached the back door of our tiny two-bedroom rental house, I could hear my parents' raised voices. I knew they were fighting. Even though I hated hearing them argue, it was not unusual.

I grabbed the doorknob, making sure not to make a sound, and opened it a couple of inches to see which room they were in. To my horror, not only were they in the kitchen, but Dad's eyes locked with mine, and the rage I detected caused me to release the doorknob and stumble backward.

I'm not sure how he moved so fast, but before I could make it off the back steps, he had me by the arm with one hand while his other reached for his belt. The swoosh of the belt made my hair stand on end. I knew what was next. Pain.

He beat me—there in the kitchen—while Mom watched and cried. I lost control of my bladder and my dignity on that kitchen floor. I had no idea what I had done wrong, but over the noise of my screaming and Dad yelling, I heard him say, "This will teach you not to eavesdrop again!"

I didn't know what the word "eavesdrop" meant. I just knew it was something awful I had done, and I never wanted to make that mistake again.

———

Maw-Maw Lormand was very disciplined and controlled every area of her life except her tongue. She told me things about people that I should never have known. Every "secret" she shared with me was preceded by my promise not to tell anyone.

She had her list of sins that would send people to hell. At the top of that list was "not wearing a slip." Maw-Maw preached that every female who didn't wear a slip would "bust hell wide open." Though she had boxes of beautiful new slips under her bed, she usually wore the same threadbare white one under her modest dresses.

Keeping her secrets became a problem when she began talking about my mother. It was apparent to me that she didn't like my mother very much and criticized her often. In Maw-Maw's words, my mom was "lazy, uneducated, and filthy."

When my parents moved us from one rented house to the next, Maw-Maw informed me that we had been evicted. I had never heard that word, so I asked my mom what it meant. Mom's face got very red. She and Dad got into a huge fight, and I didn't go to Maw-Maw's house again for a while.

I looked up the word one day at school and realized it was very probable that we had been evicted. Our house was nasty.

The smell of rats slapped you in the face when you walked in the door. My sisters and I caught baby mice and made them a home in shoe boxes. We fed, petted, and confined them until they learned to chew their way to freedom. Evidence of their existence was swept up on Saturdays when we cleaned the house. Roaches ran for cover when a light was turned on in any room.

One evening, an evangelist was eating supper with us after church. While we were sitting around the table visiting, a couple of roaches crawled out from the molding near the ceiling. Embarrassed, my mom grabbed a can of roach repellant from under the sink and sprayed the visible bugs. The critters surrendered, falling on their backs on the kitchen floor, legs waving slowly like they were ushering in the death angel.

My dad took charge of the annihilation process, stood on a chair and sprayed along the crack where the two unwelcome guests had entered. Within seconds, the Roach National Guard troops invaded our kitchen, covering the ceiling with black-and-brown armor.

I couldn't look at the evangelist's face. I didn't want to see the look of disgust I was sure he wore, a look I had seen enough on my grandmother's face and heard it in her tone as she spoke of our home.

Occasionally, I spent time at a friend's home. But I didn't invite them to mine. I was ashamed of it. Maw-Maw said people talked about how dirty our house was, and I believed her. I couldn't bear the thought of my friends knowing how nasty it was.

When I stayed with Maw-Maw Lormand, we got up early, and she cooked breakfast. Breakfast was always the highlight of my stay there. If I was the only one with her, I could request anything on the menu, and she would make it. French toast, or *"pain perdu,"* was my favorite.

After the breakfast dishes were clean and chores were done, we would "go visiting." Maw-Maw would bring food or homegrown vegetables to her neighbors and friends. I tagged along, hoping that her friends would have grandchildren my age.

One morning, she informed me that we were going to welcome new neighbors. The possibility of a family with children living close to her house in the country had me racing to the car. I bounced up and down on the passenger side of the front seat until Maw-Maw asked if I had ants in my pants. I grinned and tried to control my excitement.

My excitement was short lived. As we headed up the sidewalk to the home, she turned to me and instructed, "Cover your chin with your hand."

I looked at her, confused.

She repeated her command as she demonstrated with her free hand. "You put your hand over your mouth until your index finger touches your bottom lip and let the rest of your fingers cover your chin. Your palm will hide the scars on your neck. Then people won't stare at you."

I followed her instructions, and once satisfied that the scars were hidden, we continued to the door. The rest of the visit went by in a blur as I sat and held my hand to my chin. When my arm got tired, I slumped down to rest my elbow on my knee.

The "hand-to-chin" face covering was required from that day forward. Within a short time, it became a reflex. My scars were shameful. I had to hide them to be accepted.

Maw-Maw Lormand became our church's "youth leader" when I was around eleven or twelve years old. We would have "youth service" on Sunday nights at 5 p.m., one hour before church began. The preteens and teens sat in the first couple of pews, and the adults who brought them sat toward the back or stepped outside to visit.

This time was usually spent playing games that helped us memorize a Scripture verse or learn a story from the Bible. My favorite game was "Sword Drill." Maw-Maw called out a Scripture—book of the Bible, chapter, and verse—we raced to look it up and hurry to stand and begin reading it. The first person to start speaking the correct verse received a point. I was good at that game.

A game I did not enjoy was "Bible Story Pantomimes." Maw-Maw Lormand paired us up for this game and assigned each team a Bible story. Then, she sent us, one team at a time, to a room in the back to strategize our performance.

She would let the older kids be the team captains and choose their partners. The captain who chose me most of the time was a boy who was almost five years older than me. His dad was a minister in our church, and he was smart, a great actor, and attractive. The first time he chose me, I was thrilled to be picked to be his partner. I was in junior high, and he was in high school!

But when we got in the back, I learned that our performance for the game was not his primary objective. Molesting me was. He turned off the light, picked me up, and sat me in his lap, explaining that no one would love me because of my appearance. His interest in me was his "gift" for all that I would miss out on because of my "condition."

Sitting in the dark in the back room of our church while he touched me inappropriately and manipulated me into thinking he was doing me a favor was one of the most shameful experiences of my childhood.

I knew what he was doing was wrong, but I was convinced no one would believe me if I told them. My sisters' experiences with pedophiles in our church had taught me that.

When my sisters confided in my parents about being touched inappropriately, they were given a lecture about how to dress and sit and were warned against sitting in the lap of an adult male. Charges were not filed. The offender was not reprimanded or refused access to our church or to us.

We learned quickly Dad was more concerned about numbers (attendance) than numb-ers (stolen innocence).

At the close of many Sunday evening services, I went to the altar and begged God to forgive me. My offender would come and pray for me. In my childish thinking, I decided if he wasn't repenting, then I was the one sinning. The feeling of shame was so heavy that I evaded every other effort by other predators. When my maternal grandmother's husband (my step-grandfather) attempted to touch me inappropriately, I slapped him as hard as I could and ran out of the room.

Fearing that no one would believe me or that I would get in trouble, I did not tell anyone of the incident. This allowed him the opportunity to be inappropriate with my youngest siblings. When my parents learned of it, they told my grandmother. She kicked him out of her house immediately, but no legal action was taken.

My guilt and shame became heavier.

12

UNASHAMED

My face became a billboard of God's grace.

There's no pain like mouth pain. I've broken an ankle, stepped on a nail, given birth to two children, and had a toenail ripped off twice. None of these compared to the pain I've experienced on the inside of my mouth. I remember toothaches that kept me up all night with a heating pad on my face. After that reconstructive surgery creating my gumline, one grain of cooked rice felt like a knife cutting through the swollen flesh. The pain was excruciating.

But the mouth pain I'm addressing here is inflicted by us. By our words, we create pain or peace. I covered this topic in a previous chapter, but I want to drill it home.

In elementary school, there was a saying that we used in arguments that is untrue. The phrase was most often used when another child called you names or said something unkind about you. If you delivered the words, you said it matter-of-factly, probably with your hands on your hips. The phrase?

> *Sticks and stones may break my bones,*
> *but words can never hurt me.*

As I grew up, I realized how false this saying was. Words said to me by my father and other adults had taken up residence in my heart. I played their words repeatedly until I believed them. This practice created a miserable person.

As sensorimotor neuroscientist Dr. E. Paul Zehr shares in *Psychology Today*, "It doesn't matter whether our brains get information from our skin, our ears, our eyes, or our thoughts; hurtful intentions can cause pain." (Zehr 2023)

I have firsthand knowledge that what Zehr wrote is true.

While listening to a motivational podcast by Terri Savelle Foy, I heard that phrase reworded, "Sticks and stones may break my bones, but my words have the ability to shatter my dreams or secure my success." (Foy 2020)

Early one morning during my devotion, a Scripture leaped out at me. Found in Proverbs 12:14 (KJV), it states, "A man shall be satisfied with good by the fruit of his mouth."

As I read and reread that Scripture, I felt God asked me, "Could you survive on the fruit of your mouth? What 'side effects' are your words having on your mind, body, and spirit? Is it time to go on a word diet?"

Now, I've always loved to exercise, but I cringe at the thought of a diet or having to go for long periods without my sugar fix. For years, I watched my mom diet. It held no appeal.

The first diet I remember her trying was Weight Watchers. Other diets she tried over the years included the grapefruit diet, the Cookie Diet, and SlimFast.

The cabbage soup diet of the eighties was one I joined my mother in doing. I was engaged to be married and wanted to look stunning in my wedding dress. Other people I knew had tried it and lost as much as ten pounds in ONE week!

This diet required you to eat (if you can call it that) only cabbage soup for seven days. I'm pretty sure I gave up around day three or four. I was starving to death. Later, we found out that you only lost water and muscle mass. And as soon as you started eating regular food, the weight returned.

Other diets I remember were the Beverly Hills Diet, the Jenny Craig diet, the Atkins Diet, Nutrisystem, and the South Beach Diet. When that last one was popular, you were "cool" if you had that book sitting in plain sight in your home or office.

Regardless of the name of the diet, each one listed certain foods that were the enemy of your health. All promised weight loss if you followed their restrictive diet.

I understood this with food but never applied this concept to my words. Even the healthiest foods, if eaten in excess, may cause weight gain. But healthy words may be consumed in massive portions several times daily, with no adverse effects. And I found the Bible has a lot to say about them.

Proverbs 13:2 (KJV) says, "A man shall eat GOOD by the FRUIT of his mouth; but the soul of the transgressors shall eat violence."

Proverbs 13:3 (KJV) reports, "He that keepeth his mouth [or watches his diet of words] keepeth his life; but he that openeth wide his lips [says everything he is feeling or thinking] shall have destruction."

Don't ignore your negativity thinking it will go away.

1 Peter 3:10 (KJV) reinforces this concept: "For he that will love life, and see good days, let him refrain his tongue from evil, and his lips that they speak no guile."

Lastly, Proverbs 15:4 (AMP) tells us, "A soothing tongue [speaking words that build up and encourage] is a tree of life, but a perversive tongue [speaking words that overwhelm and depress] crushes the spirit."

In other words, if you want to live a healthy life, put your WORDS on a DIET.

To help us remember this concept, I made an acronym out of the word "WORD."

The **"W"** stands for **WHAT ARE YOU SAYING?**

The first thing we need to do is listen to what we are saying and figure out why we are saying it. ESPECIALLY IF IT IS NEGATIVE. Don't ignore your negativity and think it will go away.

Avoid absolute phrases like "I will never" or "I can't."

Example: "Things never go my way!"

If negative things always happen to us, maybe we are inviting them into our spaces. And when using the word never, remember that it means never, not one time, ever. Could this mean that we are unthankful when we fail to acknowledge the positive, good things in our lives but are quick to point out the bad?

The Bible tells us, "Out of the abundance of the heart, the mouth speaks" (Luke 6:45 KJV). Your words give listeners an audible picture of your heart. If you said it, even if you were joking, it came from your heart.

Negative words tell us there is something inside of us that we need to work on. For me, it was low self-esteem and unforgiveness. For years, I lived with the unhealthy condition of my heart because I didn't know I could use my words to attack it.

Just like with a food diet, where we must be conscious of what foods we are ingesting, we have to watch the words coming out of our mouths. These words are the fruit that our mind and spirit feast on. Instead of saying, "I can't," say, "I haven't figured out how to do it yet, but I will!"

I saw a post on social media that read, "Of all the people on the planet, you talk to yourself more than anyone. Make sure you are saying the right things!"

The **"O"** stands for **OWN UP TO YOUR PART** in this process.

Stop using your words to blame others or circumstances for the problems in your life. My husband came up with the saying, "Blame is spelled 'B-Lame.' As long as you are blaming other people for your problems, you are handicapping yourself."

YOU ARE THE PROBLEM, and YOU ARE THE SOLUTION! That should put a smile on your face.

In 2 Chronicles 7 (KJV), King Solomon completes the building of the house of the Lord and during the night, the Lord appears to him. In verses 13–14, the Lord tells Solomon, "If I shut up heaven that there be no rain, or if I command the locusts to devour the land, or if I send pestilence among my people;

If my people, which are called by my name, shall humble themselves, and pray, and seek my face, and turn from their wicked ways; then will I hear from heaven, and will forgive their sin, and will heal their land."

When things seem to come against us, instead of using your words to complain, use them to humble yourself, pray, and seek His face. That's God's recipe for success.

The recipe comes out right every time. There is a difference between asking for help and whining and complaining. In my opinion, whining and complaining are the atheistic fruits of our lips. It's our admittance that God either cannot or will not come to our aid.

Philippians 4:6 (KJV) tells us how to approach God with our problems: "Be careful for nothing; but in every thing by prayer and supplication with thanksgiving let your requests be made known unto God."

The above verse in The Message version says, "Don't fret or worry. Instead of worrying, pray. Let petitions and praises shape your worries into prayers, letting God know your concerns. Before you know it, a sense of God's wholeness, everything coming together for good, will come and settle you down. It's wonderful what happens when Christ displaces worry at the center of your life."

In other words, our problems will become our praise.

The **"R"** stands for **READ HIS WORD.**

The Bible is the best motivational book there is. 99.9% of the content of motivational books is reworded Scriptures. Phrases like "Go to your happy place" and positive meditations are directives from Philippians 4:8 (KJV), which says, "Finally, brethren, whatsoever things are true, whatsoever things are honest, whatsoever things are just, whatsoever things are pure, whatsoever things are lovely, whatsoever things are of good report; if there be any virtue, and if there be any praise, think on these things."

God is the original motivational speaker!

Finally, the **"D"** stands for **DECIDE YOUR FUTURE.**

Understand this principle: your mouth directs change. What you say determines where you go.

The book of James explains this in chapter 3 (MSG): "A bit in the mouth of a horse controls the whole horse. A small rudder on a ship in the hands of a skilled captain sets a course in the face of the strongest winds. A word out of your mouth may seem of no account, but it can accomplish nearly anything—or destroy it!"

Speak life. When you speak healthy, faith-filled words, you are speaking life.

Proverbs 18:21 says, "Death and life are in the power of the tongue."

There are two things our words do. Attack and attract.

Our words have power. That's why we need to be intentional about what we say. Our words are creating something.

Isaiah 55:11 (NKJV) helps us to understand this concept: "So shall My word be that goes forth from My mouth; It shall not return to Me void, But it shall accomplish what I please, And it shall prosper in the thing for which I sent it."

We are made in His image. We send out a command whenever we speak, and by that action, we create things.

Make a covenant with yourself that you will stay on a healthy word diet from this day forward. You will speak intentionally and believe that everything you want to happen in your life *is going to happen.* It's a little scary to think we can create our demise with our words, right?

Proverbs 18:20–21 (MSG) says, "Words satisfy the mind as much as fruit does the stomach; good talk is as gratifying as a good harvest. Words kill, words give life; they're either poison or fruit—you choose."

And since we're talking about diets, you can't get fat eating healthy words. But you can lose enough weight (baggage) to fly when Jesus returns!

I struggled with my words. I labeled myself "Little Christian Paula." It wasn't long before "Little Christian Paula" became a thief and a liar. I believed I was unlovable. Therefore, I behaved as unlovable. My childhood included events that happened to me, but it wasn't until I was an adult that I learned I could control my response to them.

As Craig Groeschel shared in his leadership podcast, "You do what you do because of what you think of you." (Groeschel n.d.)

As I shared in a previous chapter, I was responsible for laundry for our family. One day, when I was putting away Dad's folded underwear, I noticed a wad of cash toward the back of the drawer. The money wasn't neatly stashed. It looked as though he had unloaded his pockets in a hurry.

As the weeks progressed, the amount of crumpled bills increased.

I was a college student at this time and rewarded myself with a shopping trip after passing an exam. During one of these shopping sprees, I spent the majority of my paycheck. After I got home and counted my change, I realized that I would run out of money for fuel at least a week before my next paycheck.

I decided to "borrow" gas money from Dad's stash. I told myself that he wouldn't notice, and I would pay it back as soon as I got paid.

But I passed another exam the next week and needed my income to reward myself. My fuel would be compliments of my father. I justified my stealing by telling myself that he owed it to me after the way he treated me. And it wasn't really stealing if I planned to pay him back.

A few months later, I overheard Dad asking one of my sisters if she had taken money from his drawer. She denied it. He questioned all of us. Using my superpower, I remained emotionless as I stared into his eyes, swearing my innocence. But I knew better than to take any more.

I applied for a credit card. After all, I owed it to myself to supply the motivation for working so hard. I was the first one in my family to graduate from college.

As the semesters passed, my credit card collection became quite impressive. This new form of currency promised savings when I used it. Who could pass up a deal like that?

By the time I got married, my credit cards no longer fit in my wallet. They were held together by a couple of medium-sized rubber bands. Most were charged to the limit, and I was only able to make the minimum payments.

My debt was almost $10,000, and I kept that information to myself. As Clifton groaned beneath the loads of clothes and shoes he carried into our first home, he had no idea the weight of debt that those clothes represented.

In the first few months of our marriage, after an argument over where our money was going, I confessed. The look of disappointment on Clifton's face made me angry. He should have understood. It wasn't my fault. I was just a "little Christian." I couldn't help myself. It was who I was, and I lived up to my label.

A spiritual spring-cleaning was desperately needed. But first, "Little Christian Paula" needed a God who was a name changer.

I found such a God in the book of Genesis. Genesis chapter 11 introduces us to Abram, who marries Sarai. In Genesis 12:1–3 (NKJV), the Lord meets with Abram and tells him, "Get out of your country, from your family and from your father's house. To a land that I will show you. I will make you a great nation; I will bless you and make your name great; and you shall be a blessing. I will bless those who bless you, and I will curse him who curses you; And in you all the families of the earth shall be blessed."

Pretty cool promise, right? History reveals Abram was around seventy-five years old at the time of that promise. During the next twenty-four years, Abram traveled through various countries. His wife, Sarai, was lovely; apparently, Abram believed she was beautiful enough to kill for. When they got to Egypt, Abram lied and said Sarai was his sister so the Pharaoh wouldn't kill him. So now Abram is a liar.

God promised Abram his descendants would be as numerous as the stars in the sky (Genesis 15:5). But the reality is he and Sarai had no children. He must have shared the promise multiple times with Sarai, who became frustrated at her lack of conception. She convinced Abram to sleep with her Egyptian handmaid, Hagar, in a devious plan to fulfill God's promise using faulty human logic and unwise intervention.

When Abram was eighty-six years old, he became the father of Ismael, Hagar's son. But this was not how God intended to make him a "great nation."

When Abram was ninety-nine years old, the Lord made another visit and told him, "I am Almighty

God; walk before Me and be blameless. And I will make My covenant between Me and you, and will multiply you exceedingly" (Genesis 17:1–2 NKJV).

Abram fell on his face (I believe he was repenting), and God not only renewed His covenant but also changed Abram's name to Abraham.

Abram means "exalted father." Abraham means "father of a multitude." Abraham also means "friend of God." The second time God promised him a multitude of descendants, He also changed Sarai's name to Sarah.

In Genesis 17:19 (PKLV), God holds a gender reveal party before the conception and announces. "It's a boy! Name him Isaac."

God promised Abraham that from this one son would come a legacy for all the generations to follow.

Notice that God promised this to a man who had failed to trust Him previously. A man who pretended to be single to protect his own skin. Not once, but twice!

And when we read further, it seems that the lying genes of Abraham and the manipulating practices of Sarah are reproduced in their sons, daughter-in-law, and grandchildren.

———

Isaac was born and when he came of age, he married Rebekah. Believing his wife was "to die for," Isaac slipped off his wedding ring before they checked into a hotel in Gerar, and his deception was uncovered after several weeks. Yet, the Lord continued to bless him.

Isaac and Rebekah had twin boys, Esau and Jacob. As the elder son, Esau was destined to inherit the majority of the family fortune. He was the one who would carry on his father's name. But Jacob wanted to rewrite the will.

Jacob drew up a power of attorney in Esau's name, giving Jacob control of the family fortune, and waited for an opportunity to get Esau to sign it.

Knowing that the way to get to a man is through his stomach, Jacob made Esau's favorite stew and had it simmering on the stove when Esau came in from work. He asked Jacob for a bowl of it and Jacob seized the opportunity to barter with him.

"I will trade you a bowl of stew for your signature."

Esau knew the document had to do with their inheritance, but his growling stomach didn't give him permission to read the fine print. Neither of them told their father of the arrangement.

A doctor's examination revealed that Isaac's health was deteriorating and organs were decreasing productivity. No one told him hospice had been called, but his hearing had increased to compensate for his lack of sight. Knowing his time on this earth was short, he called in Esau and asked for another bite of wild game. He promised to go over the will during their meal together. Esau grabbed his hunting gear and rushed to the hunt.

Rebekah overheard the conversation and immediately called Jacob. The mother and son then plotted to deceive Isaac and implement the plan.

Jacob ran outside and killed two of the family goats. Rebekah helped him butcher them and she prepared the food in the instant pot. While the meat was simmering, she created a costume for him with the skin from the goats. (Esau was hairy and Jacob was smooth skinned.)

When Jacob entered his father's room and addressed him, Isaac asked, "Who are you?" and questioned how the food came so quickly. Jacob concocted a story, which made Isaac suspicious. Maybe because he knew all too well the behavior of a liar. After all, he was a deceiver by name and nature.

Isaac had Jacob come close enough to touch him and he then rubbed Jacob's arms. I'm sure Jacob broke into a cold sweat and was grateful for his "goatskin gloves."

After the examination, Isaac was still suspicious. "The voice is Jacob's voice, but the hands are the hands of Esau. Are you really my son Esau?"

The lies multiply as Jacob responds, "I am."

Even though Isaac knew the voice didn't sound like Esau, he trusted what he felt. Holding Jacob's arm with one hand, he signed the will and initialed the power of attorney form.

And there you have it. This story perfectly exemplifies what happens when we trust what we feel over what we know. (Genesis 27:22, 24 PKLV)

Jacob got what he desired, but it didn't come with the euphoria he expected. His name meant "supplanter," meaning "one who wrongfully or illegally seizes and holds the place of another." He had lived up to his "label" and his success was soon replaced with shame.

Not long after Jacob left Isaac's side, Esau came carrying the meat he had killed and cooked on the backyard grill. Isaac became confused and asked for the second time that day, "Who are you?" (v. 32) When the two men realized what happened, Esau begged his father to call the family attorney. But it was too late. The paperwork had been signed by the judge and filed. Esau received the inheritance intended for Jacob.

Esau was livid with his brother and vowed to himself that after the funeral was over, he would kill Jacob.

Rebekah discovered Esau's vow concerning Jacob, so she bought him a one-way ticket and sent him to live with her brother.

Fast-forward the story several years later, Jacob now had two wives and several children and decided to return home. Jacob emailed his old friends to let them know he was coming home. He asked one of them to let his brother know.

The next day, he got a text from that friend saying Esau was on his way to meet Jacob and had four hundred men accompanying him. When Jacob heard this, he became anxious and scared for his life.

Then Jacob prayed. In Genesis 32:9, Jacob calls on the God of his grandfather, Abraham, and the God of his father, Isaac. He humbled himself and prayed for deliverance from the hand of his brother. He told God exactly how afraid he was and then reminded God of His promise to his grandfather. "You said, 'I will surely treat you well and make your descendants as the sand of the sea, which cannot be numbered for multitude.'"

In other words, Jacob was pleading, "We can't multiply if we are not alive! And I'm glad you were my father and grandfather's God. But right now, I need you to be my God too."

When you read God's Word and repeat His promises back to Him, it's called *prayer*. And when you claim those written promises in His Word, you are claiming Him as *your* God.

———

The night before he met his brother face-to-face, Jacob separated himself from his family and spent the night alone. Or so he thought. Genesis 32:24 says, "A man wrestled with him until the breaking of day."

Believing he had hold of an angel, Jacob refused to release him. Jacob understood this was a supernatural visitation, and he was not about to let the moment slip by without a significant change in himself.

Scriptures say the man wrestling with Jacob even pushed Jacob's hip out of joint to get him to let go, but Jacob held on tightly. Finally, the man said, "Let me go. It's almost morning."

Jacob replied, "I will not let you go until you bless me."

"What is your name?" asked the man.

Jacob responded, "Jacob."

Jacob, the deceiver, the one who lied to his father and stole from his brother, was confessing his character.

What he asked for was a blessing. What blessing did he want? He was in possession of his brother's inheritance. He was already a wealthy man. A promise of a long life, maybe? Since he was fearful that his brother was coming with a four-hundred-man army to kill him.

The blessing he received was a new name and a new identity.

The man replied, "Your name shall no longer be called Jacob, but Israel; for you have struggled with God and men and have prevailed."

You would think that when God talks about Jacob in the future, He would call him by his new name, right? But over and over in the following Bible books, we see God referred to as "the God of Abraham, Isaac, and Jacob." A few times, God is referred to as "the God of Abraham, Isaac, and Israel." But you will not find God referring to Abraham's old name, Abram. He stays consistent.

Only with Jacob does He go back and forth from Jacob to Israel.

I'm not sure exactly why, and the Bible doesn't explain it either, so I came up with my own conclusion: it's to let us know that He is the God of us even before we receive a new name. He is the God of our old identity. He was the God of Jacob long before Jacob decided to stop deceiving, stealing, and lying.

During my spiritual character spring-cleaning, I sat down with Clifton, and we performed plastic surgery. We cut up every credit card in my possession. The only cards we agreed to keep were our Visa and American Express. Those were joint accounts, and Clifton had full access to those records. No more lying and stealing. But above all, NO MORE GUILT.

Well, almost none. I knew I still owed my father. So, I cashed a check, sat down, and wrote my dad a letter, admitting to taking his money. I mailed that letter and the cash I owed him, and as I dropped it into the mail, the guilt I had been carrying around for years fell with it. I had finally come clean.

Several days later, I received a letter from my dad. In it, he wrote that he forgave me. The letter included all the cash I had sent. The debt was canceled. I was no longer Paula, the little Christian, the liar, the thief, and the manipulator. I was no longer *Paula the Victim*. I became *Paula the Victor*.

I want to pause and go back in time.

Dad moved our family to Jennings in 1970. As I wrote before, our church was very small—fewer than twenty people—during that first year. But the following July, Dad brought the family to our organization's church camp in Tioga, Louisiana. There, hundreds of churches gathered annually for service. The tabernacle was huge, and the platform was high. When I was there, I felt like I was part of something big.

On the stage were talented musicians and singers, dressed in the most beautiful clothes. They all looked as impressive as the building itself.

I was eight years old at the time. I remember sitting in that vast auditorium with thousands of people and looking up at the platform and thinking, "How cool would it be to be up there?"

The meeting lasted a week and, on the ride home, I shared my thoughts with the two sisters closest in age to me. They nodded their heads in agreement. The three of us had been singing in our tiny church for the past year. We giggled and planned our wardrobe in case the opportunity to sing in front of thousands ever presented itself. My dad interrupted our daydream and shattered our hopes with his words, "You have to have been born on that platform in order to be on it."

I was old enough to know what he meant. During the past week, when our family was alone in the single hotel room, he would talk badly about the speakers and how much better he could have done. The music was not up to his standard either. He could have fixed it all if they would only give him a voice. But no one wanted to listen to him.

He convinced himself (and us) that you had to belong to the right family in order to be used in a statewide event in our church organization. From his comment in the vehicle, it was obvious that our family did not have the right name.

The next summer, while at camp, I did a little investigating and learned that the two favored names in our organization in the state of Louisiana were Tenney and Mangun. The only chance I had of taking on one of those names was through marriage or adoption. I figured adoption was out, so I began inquiring about the availability of sons. Both of their sons were too old for me and were already married.

I would have to accept the fact that I would never be a member of the right family.

As I got older, I decided that if I couldn't become a Tenney or a Mangun, I would do my best to look and act like them.

I couldn't figure out how to do my hair like Thetus Tenney or Vesta Mangun, so I copied Vesta's daughter-in-law, Mickey Mangun. I wore my hair slicked back in a neat bun.

Vesta played an accordion, but when I attempted to play as she did, I realized that the instrument was too heavy for me. I almost had to stand on one end of it to pull it apart.

Next, I took piano lessons, determined to play like Mickey. I learned a few chords, five to be exact. But my attempts at playing and singing sounded more like a howling dog concert than worship.

I was terrified to pray in public because I thought I should sound like Vesta. After fifteen to twenty seconds, I would stop, believing I was a disgrace to God and my family.

I offered to teach the adult class. But when my lessons didn't contain as much wisdom as Thetus Tenney's, I felt like a failure.

I was doomed to be just plain Paula Kristine LeJeune.

God had other plans. In 2008, I was invited to be a part of a group of pastors' wives led by Thetus Tenney. At the first meeting, I was starstruck at being at the same table with Mickey Mangun AND Thetus Tenney. Other women in the group were ones I had admired but had little or no relationship with. I sat through the entire event saying little but learning a lot.

Thetus Tenney felt I belonged at that table, and I was determined not to let her down. I borrowed her confidence until I developed my own. I began stretching myself and offering to teach classes in our church. I approached new members of our congregation and offered to teach them Bible studies.

The old Paula was a victim and expected rejection. But the new Paula decided that people needed to know me, and I wanted to develop new relationships. My offers were accepted, and God began opening doors for me to continue to grow.

The next year, a couple of days before my forty-sixth birthday, Thetus Tenney called me and asked if I would be available to drive her to a conference she wanted to attend. Her husband was supposed to drive her, but the death of a pastor friend had changed their plans.

Of course, I said, "Yes!"

On my birthday, I drove Thetus Tenney to that conference. When we walked in, we were greeted and directed to a table to pick up our name tags and packets. Thetus Tenney was given her name tag, and I was handed a lanyard that read, "T. F. Tenney."

The administrator offered to write my name on another tag, but I shook my head and smiled. "I'll wear his."

I was seated in the front row next to Thetus. It was a seat of honor. I was treated with all of the dignity and respect T. F. Tenney would have received, and I enjoyed every minute of it.

Spending my birthday as T. F. Tenney was the best birthday gift!

Five months later, I received a phone call from the pastor's wife of the church that hosted the conference I had attended as T. F. Tenney. The call came on a Thursday afternoon. The pastor's wife was desperate to find a speaker for the following night's women's event.

She explained that the scheduled speaker had to cancel at the last minute, and her ladies' committee had decided that I would be a good replacement for the speaker. On that Friday evening, I walked onto the platform to speak to a full-capacity crowd who was there to hear Mickey Mangun.

Since then, I have been on the Louisiana District campground platform more times than I can count. Each time I ascended those platform steps, my dad's voice faded just a little more. Until the memory of his harsh rhetoric became a whisper easily drowned by the encouragement of a God whose voice determines our futures.

God doesn't play. If you need a new name, He will provide you with one until you can make a new name for yourself. I no longer have to be ashamed of who I am, nor do I need to frustrate myself trying to be someone else.

He is proud to be the God of Abraham, Isaac, Jacob, and *Paula*.

THE CONFLICT

God loves you just the way you are,
but he refuses to leave you that way.

Max Lucado

When I was a child, I thought like a child,
I reasoned like a child.
When I became a man,
I put the ways of childhood behind me

(1 Corinthians 13:11 NIV).

13

NORMAL CHAOS

I grew up in a messy house. Although Mom knew how to clean, she was not good at keeping it clean. Maybe she was overwhelmed or overworked, but whatever her excuse, our house stayed in disarray.

We left our home in chaos every morning, and that chaos greeted us every afternoon as we returned from school. From the time I was in first grade, before starting homework, my sisters and I had to clean the house. Our chores included washing the dishes caked with dried-out food we had eaten the night before, making all of the beds—including my parents' bed, sweeping and mopping floors, and folding any laundry left in the dryer.

Our duties increased as we got older, which meant that homework had to be pushed back until after supper if it was done at all. When I was in high school, I would often set my alarm for 4 a.m. in order to complete assignments. I was a morning person and couldn't concentrate at night.

Laundry piles were part of the decoration in our house. And not just near the washing machine.

Piles of laundry could be found in bathrooms and bedrooms, and a mountain of clean laundry seemed to be the main attraction in the living room. Saturdays were spent changing the landscape. Before going to bed on Saturday evening, every mountain had been conquered.

All of our efforts seemed futile when, within twenty-four hours, clutter covered tables, chairs, and the floor. It was a vicious cycle and a lifestyle I hated.

The volatile behavior of my parents intensified the chaos. When either was angry, their behavior regressed to that of a preteen, yelling obscenities and harsh words while hurling objects through the air. Sometimes the items were aimed at a target. Other times, the only purpose was destruction.

After the tantrum ended, my sisters and I were required to clean up the mess. After the evidence was removed, everyone pretended it never happened.

But sometimes, we got a break…

Dad had taken a motorcycle trip, and for a few days, we were able to play after our chores were done. Knowing we were experiencing a vacation of sorts, Mom hesitantly asked for our help repainting and sprucing up her bedroom. We responded to the invitation like it was a trip to a theme park. Helping Mom would make her smile, and she had a beautiful smile.

The room took on a festive atmosphere as we bounced around the room, rearranging furniture, cleaning the nightstands and the dresser, organizing drawers, and making her room look as clean and beautiful as possible in the presence of faded curtains and worn wooden floors.

Dad returned from his trip, and Mom proudly showed him what we had accomplished. We followed behind her, eagerly awaiting his positive response. When he viewed his side of the room, his face changed from an agreeable smile to one of intense anger.

"Where did you move all of my stuff?" he demanded.

As Mom stuttered to answer him, he began throwing things around the room. I ran down the steps to hide. My sisters did the same.

The thin walls did little to muffle their voices. Mom was screaming something about wanting a clean house, and Dad was yelling at her not to touch his stuff. We covered our ears and stayed hidden.

It wasn't long before we heard his heavy boots descending the stairs, followed by Mom's cries, begging him not to leave. I wanted to shove him out and lock the door, but I knew better. I stayed crouched between the legs of chairs underneath the dining table.

He marched from room to room, grabbing shotguns lounging in corners and pistols stashed in drawers, and headed for the door. Before exiting, he announced that it was obvious we didn't want him around, and he was heading into the woods to kill himself.

This wasn't the first time he had threatened to kill himself. And it wasn't the first time he had left, promising not to return. He always, eventually, came back. It seemed the only promises he could keep were the ones where we would feel pain.

The closest wooded area was in Evangeline, where Dad's childhood home still stood. Mom figured that was where he would go. She phoned the sheriff of Acadia parish, who promised to go out and look for him, but he didn't sound hopeful. Dad knew the wooded area in Evangeline better than most of the deputies. If he wanted solitude, he knew where to find it. The creases in Mom's forehead deepened as she and the sheriff spoke, and her eyes glazed over as she set the phone back in its cradle. She didn't cook supper. She didn't do anything except sit next to the phone and cry.

She couldn't afford to support us. She had nowhere to go. She didn't know where Dad had gone, so she couldn't go out and look for him.

Jonette, Trudy, and I did our best to comfort her while taking care of five-year-old Terri Jo and two-year-old Laura. We fixed ourselves something to eat and put the little ones to bed. Then we stationed ourselves on the floor of Mom's bedroom, lying on makeshift pallets of threadbare blankets and worn pillows.

Around 2 a.m., the phone rang, shrilly piercing the silence. Jonette got to it first. It was Dad. She held the phone away from her ear so we could hear him.

Dad was still in a rage, but it was a quiet, controlled one. He wanted us to know that he still planned to kill himself and even clicked the gun a few times so we would understand how serious he was. Mom was sobbing, and the three of us began screaming, begging him not to take his life.

We promised not to touch his stuff if he just would come home.

Dad would say, "Ya'll don't love me."

We were devastated that he could think that. And we wailed, "We do love you, Daddy! Please come home!"

He made us repeat it several times before he hung up on us. None of us could sink back into the safety of sleep. Our minds raced, and our bodies refused to relax as we strained to hear his vehicle pull into the driveway. We waited through the night, anticipating his return or a call from the police stating his body had been found.

He returned none the worse for wear and repeated this action several times whenever he warranted the circumstances called for it. He would disappear for days before the expected phone call. We would plead with him. He would return. It was never discussed. With anyone.

We became experts at normalizing abnormal behavior.

14

CREATING CHAOS

Ten years before I was born, DNA was discovered. At that time, scientists concluded that we were victims of our genetics.

Genetics determined my hair color, eye color, height, the size of my hands and feet, as well as many other physical features. It also sentenced me to poor eyesight, early graying (my mom was completely gray headed by the time she was forty-five), and eventually high blood pressure.

I was a teenager when I learned about my parents' high blood pressure. I overheard them discussing the problem several times, but they never stayed consistent in controlling their eating habits. Fried and fatty foods were cooked and served repeatedly. Sunday dinner was the same for years: fried chicken, rice dressing, baked beans, and on occasion, French fries.

In science and health classes in high school, I learned that exercise and eating habits could make a difference in high blood pressure. So, I became proactive about exercising. While I lived at home, I did not have a lot of control over the foods I ate, but I did have a choice over how much I consumed.

Before I was twenty years old, my father had his first heart attack. I remember lying in my bed at the end of the single-wide trailer house where we lived at the time and hearing my dad crying out in pain in the living room. The walls were thin, and he may as well have been sitting in my room. I could hear every moan and groan as he wrestled with the pain. He was stubborn, and it was morning before Mom convinced him to go to the hospital.

A few tests revealed that not only had he had a heart attack, but he had four severely blocked arteries. Two days later, the doctor performed a quadruple bypass on him, and the recovery seemed as painful as the heart attack.

Watching him suffer made me even more determined to find a way to become healthier.

While Mom never had a heart attack, she had episodes where her blood pressure spiked, giving her severe headaches. Her weight would fluctuate, and it seemed she was either on a diet or talking about starting one.

My limited education taught me that this would be my lot in life. However, I was determined to do all I could to change the outcome of the poor genes that inhabited my frame. Exercise became a way of life in college. If I was offered an elective class, I would choose something physical, like racquetball, aerobics, or tennis.

I counted calories and carbs, avoided fast-food restaurants, and stayed as slim as possible. Yet, I was still diagnosed with high blood pressure at the age of forty-two.

Along with physical genetics, I inherited mental genetics. I'm not sure that all the mental stuff was really handed down to me through my genes or if it was learned behavior, but still, I had it.

I've already shared my dad's anger issues and how he could go from calm to rage in a short period of time. But Mom had anger issues also. When Mom was angry, she stayed angry for a *long* time.

————

Mom owned her own accounting business, including the building. However, there was no parking lot for her building. Everyone parked along the street. But Mom believed she owned the part of the street located in front of her office.

She became angry if she arrived at work and someone had parked in her spot. Sometimes, she would find somewhere else to park, but if she was already in a bad mood, she would park her car in the middle of the street, slam into the office, and throw her keys at one of her employees—me, when I was working there—and tell us to park it for her.

Regardless of her decision, most of her day was spent in isolation. The slamming of her office door screamed, "Do not disturb!"

When Mom and Dad would fight at home, Mom would often lock herself in her bedroom and be unavailable to us for hours. Several times, one or both would storm out of the house, get into their vehicle, and leave. We never knew if they would be gone for hours or days.

When I got married, that behavior was one I was fantastic at duplicating. If I was angry, I would either explode with hurtful, ugly words or go into my room and slam the door, daring Clifton to venture into my pity party. My mental DNA allowed me to express my anger for as long as it took to make my husband look as miserable as I felt.

When my daughters were older, I began to manipulate them with the same terrible behavior. They were victims of slamming doors and irrational anger.

During one of these "episodes," I left the house without telling them where I was going or when I would return.

———

It was July of 2014. My mom had passed away in May, and our church was in the middle of a capital stewardship campaign. I was working long hours at the church office, getting financial papers in order for the lender. I went home for lunch and found my husband and daughters sitting around the kitchen table enjoying themselves.

No one had fixed anything for me. Of course, I hadn't asked them to, but that's beside the point. How dare they have fun while I was working! They had even dared to go for a swim before lunch!

Our one-year-old fur baby, Evie, ran to me and scratched at my leg, begging to go for a walk. She was not fully potty trained yet, so I asked if anyone had walked her recently. My question was met with blank stares, which infuriated me even more. I ignored their offers to walk her, slapped the leash on to her collar, and stormed out of the door.

It was a hundred trillion degrees outside, and within seconds, I was covered in sweat. The anger boiling inside of me was more intense than the rays of the sun. I stomped around our neighborhood until Evie decided to head back to the house. By this time, my anger matched that of a mentally disturbed hornet.

I fixed a sandwich for myself, grabbed a bag of chips and a bottle of water, and walked out without speaking to any of them. Before driving out of the driveway, I placed my phone on airplane mode so they would be unable to reach me or track me on the Life 360 app we all had on our phones.

I drove to a nearby park and sat and cried. My tears soaked the bread of the sandwich that lay on my lap. I was repeating the actions of my parents. I was the one hurting my husband and children.

As I sat there, the memories of me as a child—being scared because my parents were gone and not knowing what to do—began replaying in my mind.

What kind of person had I become? Why would I want my children and husband to feel that level of torment?

My sobs grew deeper as wave after wave of guilt washed over me.

Knowing I would be unintelligible if I tried to speak with them, I sent each of them a text, letting them know where I was and how sorry I was. But I knew that a text with an apology would not be sufficient for me. If I was going to break this cycle, I would have to face them and acknowledge what I had done. When I gained control of my emotions, I returned home.

We held a family meeting in the living room, and I asked for their forgiveness. For the record, the apology process is very painful for me. I hate admitting that I am wrong. But I knew it was necessary. If I was going to change, I had to own up to my terrible actions.

To quote Dr. Sharon Martin, "We repeat what we do not repair." (Martin 2021)

I was the one who created emotional chaos by filling my brain with every inadequacy life had thrown at me. The visible scars, the abuse in my childhood, the lack of money and social status, and the absence of a safe place growing up consumed my thoughts and justified my actions.

On October 1, 2019, my emotional chaos spilled into my home, but this time I came away with clarity and a new perspective.

Cliff had worked at the church all day, Eryn had classes at the university, and my day was spent working on a message for a ladies' event scheduled for the following weekend. I was one of the speakers. I knew my topic but struggled to get my thoughts down on paper. Just when the words began to flow, I glanced at the clock and saw it was time for me to begin cooking our evening meal.

Frustrated, I entered the kitchen and began pulling out ingredients, cookware, and utensils. The angry little girl in me, the victim of her circumstances, resurfaced in my fifty-six-year-old brain.

My thoughts went something like this.

"Why do I have to stop working on something important to make sure my family is fed?

"The family members who live under my roof have the ability to cook. Neither one of them is worried about what I will eat for supper! Why me?"

I knew I could have ordered from a restaurant and continued to work. My family would have understood and not complained. But I would rather have applause for being an overachiever than admit I could not handle something as simple as preparing a meal.

I banged pots and slammed cabinets as I prepared rice dressing, baked beans, and BBQ ribs (in the oven). My canine audience walked over to her empty bowl and glared at me, making me even angrier.

"Of course! I have to feed you too!" I snapped as I filled her dish with a cup of dry dog food.

A few minutes later, Clifton arrived and strolled through the door like the king of the castle. I did not bow. I did not speak. And he did not notice.

The ribs had been seasoned and cooked in the instant pot and were in a pan, waiting to be covered with BBQ sauce and roasted to perfection. I had the sauce in my hand when Cliff walked over to inspect my menu.

Using a fork, he stripped a small portion of meat from the bone and gave his unwanted opinion, "These ribs aren't seasoned nearly enough."

My anger was irrational. All of the negative things he had said about my cooking over the last thirty years of marriage began flooding my memory. My mind went back to the previous times he stood over a pot that I had been slaving over for hours and tasted the food, and, WITHOUT MY CONSENT, added seasoning, throwing more fuel on my already raging temper. ALL OF THOSE TIMES were combined with THIS TIME and became a point of contention.

I glared at him and said, "Well, you can do all of the cooking from now on. I'm done!"

I angrily slapped the BBQ sauce on the top of the ribs and slammed them into the oven. He looked at me with a puzzled look on his face, which made me even angrier. He acted as though he had no clue why I was angry. I knew he really didn't have a clue, but I continued my tirade.

"Apparently, I don't know how to season our food. It's never good enough for you.

I hope you enjoy this meal because it's the last one you'll get from me!"

The ticking of the clock on the wall heralded the seconds we were wasting as we stared at each other in complete silence.

Cliff broke the silence with his question. "Is there something else going on? You're getting way too angry over a little seasoning."

Refusing to answer and knowing he was right, I turned and faced the oven. It would have torched the oven beyond recognition if my inner rage had been a tangible force. I heard Cliff walk away, and I began talking to myself, but not with words that would calm me down. The words spewing like a volcano through my brain added to my insane anger.

"Paula, you know he ALWAYS criticizes your cooking! You NEVER cook anything right! How many times has he called from the office inquiring about supper, and when you tell him the menu, he sighs heavily? He's even had the nerve to say he didn't want it! WHO DOES HE THINK HE IS?"

My pity party continued as I inflated invisible balloons of despair,

"I had to speak last Sunday, and I have to speak this Friday and Saturday at a women's event. I can't just get up there and ramble. I have to pray and hear from God and then articulate what I feel He wants me to say in a way that makes sense.

"Clifton has an easier life. He gets up in the morning without a care and leaves to go to the office and work. MY OFFICE IS AT HOME! (Yes, I'm having a pity party about working from home. Are your eyes rolling? Such drama, right?) In between working on messages, I have to clean the house, wash the clothes, walk the dog, and cook his supper, and HE HAS THE AUDACITY TO CRITICIZE my work!"

Eryn returned from school and my silence was broken with as few words as possible to announce that dinner was served.

The pity party escalated after the meal was over, as both Clifton and Eryn had to rush out, and I was left alone cleaning the kitchen. As I loaded the dishwasher and hand-washed pots and pans, I reminded myself how terrible my life was.

Let me pause here and give you the reality of my life at that moment.

I am married to a wonderful man who provides me with everything I wish for. This is a fact. I am careful what I say around him because if I mention wanting something, he starts figuring out how to get it for me.

My daughters have graduated from college, and each purchased a home within a mile of our home. The older is married to a wonderful man who treats her like a queen. The younger is engaged to be married to a prince of a guy. Our family is close knit, and we sincerely enjoy being together as often as possible.

My custom-built home is in a very nice subdivision and is the largest in the neighborhood. It boasts of four bedrooms, three baths, three fireplaces, and extravagant details. The view from my kitchen into the backyard resembles a resort, with its kidney-shaped pool and palm trees.

I drive a luxury sedan with heated and cooled seats as well as a heated steering wheel. My husband cleans it weekly and adds fuel as needed.

Our cruise vacation is just over a month away, and I honestly cannot think of one thing I could purchase to improve my life.

Did you get the reality of where I should be focused? Good, now back to the angry little girl in the adult woman's body. Here I was throwing a gala of a pity party only it was void of attendees, balloons, and cake.

The anger bubbled up and spilled out of my mouth, "Nobody wants to help me! Nobody cares about me!"

Those were words I heard my father say when he was frustrated and angry. The dark side of Dad was one I had fought to resist duplicating, but that day, it resurrected with a vengeance.

This behavior that I had begged God to help me get rid of, had returned upon invitation. The rational woman inside of me said I was overreacting, but the adolescent victim refused to comply.

When the kitchen was cleaned to my satisfaction, I grabbed my purse and keys and headed to family prayer at my church. Yes, I went to a prayer service at the church we pastor, angry at my husband.

When the preliminaries of the prayer service were concluded, I found a secluded place to pour out my frustration. When I was through whining, God didn't send comfort into my spirit. He sent conviction about my attitude.

John 14:26 says, "But the Helper, the Holy Spirit, whom the Father will send in My name, He will teach you all things, and bring to your remembrance *all things that I said to you.*"

I've quoted that Scripture to my daughters when they were in school. They had studied for tests and when I prayed over them, I reminded them that God would bring correct answers to their remembrance on difficult questions.

But God doesn't just help us remember facts for a test. This time God began reminding me about how far He had brought me, how He had answered my prayer and delivered me from a victim mindset.

As I knelt there and wept, He sent reels skipping through my mind of the "old Paula." The Paula who shut down and punished people by not speaking to them. The Paula who spent hours plotting ways to get back at the people who had hurt her. That "old me" who I hadn't seen in a long time had just consumed over an hour of my day.

Tears soaked the cloth chair as I repented for revisiting my "old self." Before I got up, my sweet husband appeared beside me and prayed for me. He verbalized all the things I was struggling with, and I used an entire box of tissues in thirty minutes.

While the Tuesday night prayer meeting did help, I still had to apologize to my husband when we got home. Then, God and I had a long talk early the next morning. I took Him up on His offer in Matthew 11:28 (NKJV): "Come to me, all you who labor and are heavy laden, and I will give you rest."

I repented for not going to Him first. Then I asked for His help. Just as I was determined to change my physical DNA, I was equally determined to change my mental DNA. I did not know how or where to start, but I knew that the problem was within me, and if I expected a better marriage and life than my parents had, I had to *change*.

15

REDEFINING CHAOS

Your lack of joy may very well be in
what you are thinking or saying.

Joyce Meyer

The "Pity Gala" I threw for myself in the last section was not my last one, but they continued to get shorter and shorter. After that week was over, I began reflecting on why I had allowed the "old me" to resurface. I needed to figure out how I got to that point so I would recognize it *before* it happened again.

What I learned was that I am more likely to go back to my old way of thinking when (1) I'm tired, (2) I'm stressed, and (3) I'm self-absorbed or carnal.

The first two were easy to determine. The third one required more questions. The real reason I was so frustrated about writing that message was that I was focused on making myself look good instead of focusing on what God wanted me to deliver.

Once I asked for His help, His thoughts flooded my brain in the order that He wanted, and the entire sermon came together seamlessly.

There's a reason Peter tells me in 1 Peter 5:8 to "Be sober and be vigilant!" I must stand guard and not allow my old nature to return.

The Scripture continues, "...because your adversary the devil walks about like a roaring lion, seeking whom he may devour."

If I don't stay sober and vigilant, my "old self" will devour the peace God helped me construct in my life. It will rob me of the life God intended for me and my family to enjoy.

What matters the most to God is not how I minister in front of an audience. He is most concerned about how I minister at home. The proof of the Holy Spirit in my life is the FRUIT of the Spirit, and the FRUIT of the Spirit should FIRST be served at HOME. I needed to become the person I would want to come home to.

In John 13:35, Jesus said, "By this all will know that you are my disciples, *if you have love for one another.*"

My gifts and talents mean nothing if I'm not treating people right. My husband taught this in our early years of pastoring, and it has become a creed in our church as well as our home.

"It is never right to treat people wrong."

Apparently, Paul had struggled with emotions similar to mine before he wrote the letter to the church in

Philippi. In Philippians 3:12–16 (MSG), Paul gets vulnerable:

> "I'm not saying that I have this all together, that I have it made. But I am well on my way, reaching out for Christ, who has so wondrously reached out for me. Friends, don't get me wrong: By no means do I count myself an expert in all of this, but I've got my eye on the goal, where God is beckoning us onward. I'm off and running, and I'm not turning back. So let's keep focused on that goal, those of us who want everything God has for us. If any of you have something else in mind, something less than total commitment, God will clear your blurred vision—you'll see it yet! Now that we're on the right track, let's stay on it!"

We can't move forward if we don't work daily to put away the mindsets of our pasts.

John 8:31–32 (NKJV) says, "If you abide in My word, you are My disciples indeed. And you shall know the truth, and the truth shall make you free."

As Joyce Meyer said in a recent podcast, "It **is** the truth that makes us free. But it's not the truth about somebody else. It's the truth about **us** that sets us free. And I think the hardest thing to deal with is the truth that all of your problems are not somebody else's faults."

As I listened to her speaking, I felt as though I was on a phone call with her, and she was lovingly correcting me. She had been hurt and abused as had I, but she spoke from a place of healing.

"It's very hard to take responsibility for your own mess," she stated.

She, like me, had justified her poor behavior as an adult on the fact that she was abused as a child. God spoke to her and said, "Yes, that's why you are the way you are, but don't let it become an excuse to stay that way."

Hours of therapy would probably not have impacted me as much as those thirty seconds of instruction from someone who had walked in my shoes and invested in a new pair. I was determined to keep the changes I had already made.

I've heard Thetus Tenney speak on the subject of "seasons" several times. Each time, I'm convicted for comparing myself with someone who is in a different season or being frustrated in the season I'm in.

Seasons change. When I held my pity party over Cliff's comment about "seasoning," I realized we were entering a new season. Eryn was engaged to be married in a couple of months. She was the only child still at home. For Cliff and me, the next season was going to be just the two of us in our home.

For much of the time, he was going to be the *only person* I had to talk to. I knew I needed to get my attitude right in this season, or the next one would be miserable. My audience wouldn't know if I was treating him right, but Cliff would.

You see, it's not about the seasoning, it's about the season. Seasoning gives flavor and makes food enticing. If my heart is not seasoned with forgiveness, love, and mercy, my family will not be able to stomach me.

———————

Three years ago, on an early morning run, I listened to Jim Rohn telling us how to go from ordinary to extraordinary. (Rohn 2021) One of the things needed to accomplish this feat was "change." Jim listed six facts we need to know about change. When I was finished with my run, I replayed the podcast and took notes.

The six facts are:

1. People change just enough to get away from their problems.

2. Most people want to change their circumstances to improve their lives instead of changing themselves to improve their circumstances.

3. Most people do the same thing the same way and expect different results.

4. Most people are willing to change—not because they see the light—but because they feel the heat. If you wait until you feel the heat, it's often too late.

5. Most people are unwilling to pay the immediate price of change; therefore, they do not change and pay the ultimate price.

6. Most people see change as a hurtful thing that must be done instead of a helpful thing that should be done.

In 1988, I got married with the mindset of the tail end of these six facts. I recognized that change was needed, but I thought that everything and everyone around me needed to change. It didn't dawn on me for years I was the one who needed to change. I knew I wanted a better life for myself, but I was convinced that my childhood and my parents were the problem. I thought the change of address would change everything about me. I couldn't have been more wrong.

I wanted to be a cycle-breaker, but when I got angry or felt sorry for myself, I repaired that old cycle and hopped back on it. When I began asking God for help, I started seeing what He desired to show me about the changes I needed to make. God is ready to show us, when we are ready to ask for His help.

Deuteronomy 30:19 says, "I call heaven and earth to record this day against you, that I have set before you life and death, blessing and cursing: therefore choose life [choose to break destructive cycles] so that both you and your children may live."

To become a cycle-breaker, I had to take responsibility for my life. I had to accept that my choices had consequences. I could control my choices, but the consequences of my choices were out of my control. Then, I asked for God's help. It really was that simple, but the changes were not quick and easy.

I've already used this Scripture in this book, but I use it again because it's been a daily prayer. James 1:5 says, "If any of you lacks wisdom, you should ask God, who gives generously to all without finding fault"— that means He won't think it's a dumb question—"and it will be given you."

Take God at His Word. It works.

———

My childhood Christmases are not good memories. So many holidays were ruined because one or both of my parents would get angry and compete in a screaming match or storm out of the house. I remember getting a whipping on the side of the road somewhere in between Jennings and Kinder one Christmas Eve because my sisters and I were arguing in the back seat while my parents argued in the front. Our arguing agitated my dad enough for him to pull over and "convince" us to stop.

We usually spent Christmas Eve with my mom's mom, but if Dad were in one of his moods, the slightest provocation caused him to turn the car around and head back home. Whether it was an argument or a canceled Christmas, whenever my parents would calm down, the incident was never discussed. We just had to pretend it didn't happen.

I think that is the reason I go all out for Christmas. Every room in my house gets decorated. At least six trees are set up, and even the chalk wall in the kitchen wears a six foot or taller Christmas tree drawing. I'm determined to replace terrible Christmases with good ones.

As I was growing up, Dad preached about the love of God and His mercy, but I quickly recognized that he didn't truly understand it. It was a concept I didn't get until I was married and had children. When I began seeking God's guidance to be a cycle-breaker, He led me to 1 Corinthians, chapter 13.

Now, you can go back and read through the entire chapter in whatever version you are comfortable with, but as I studied it, I rewrote it.

So this is 1 Corinthians 13 in the PKLV: first, Paul jumps right into setting Spirit-filled Christians straight when he says, "Even though you can speak several languages, speak in tongues, prophesy, have faith that moves mountains, give everything you own to the poor and sacrifice your life to the point of becoming a martyr, it means *nothing* if you don't have love."

Then, he tells us what love is: "it is patient, kind, doesn't envy, and isn't prideful." Those characteristics *did not* describe my father, or me for that matter.

Next, Paul launches into the hard part: love does not behave indecently, is not demanding, is not easily provoked, and is not destructive. These are characteristics of a victim, not a born-again child of God.

These were things I worked to change. And, make no mistake, it was work. Rewarding work, but work, nonetheless. I couldn't change my past. I couldn't change my father. I could only change myself. And to change my responses, I had to change the way I thought.

If there's anything I've learned over the past decade, it's this: it is harder to think the right thing than it is to do the right thing.

To be a cycle-breaker, I had to learn to take ownership of my thoughts and my actions. 2 Corinthians 10:5 tells us that it is our responsibility to take every thought captive and make it obedient to Christ. We are not victims controlled by our thoughts. We can recognize poor thinking and change it.

As we continue reading Paul's letter, he breaks it down for us in verse 6: "love does not celebrate poor behavior, but celebrates personal excellence."

I believe that is the key to breaking a dysfunctional cycle. Stop normalizing and celebrating poor behavior. Read the previous sentence again. Take a little time to let it soak in.

To be a cycle-breaker, I had first to recognize my own poor behavior, apologize, and change. Apologizing to my husband and daughters helped me to be accountable. That is the key.

I saw an Instagram post in 2022 that read, "Being held accountable may feel like an attack if you're not ready to acknowledge how your poor decisions impact others."

When I was a child, and my parents acted like children (screamed, hollered, stormed out), once they cooled down, we just went on with life and pretended it never happened. I knew how traumatized I was and felt horrible that I was repeating their actions.

Once I decided to change, I began apologizing and discussing my poor behavior. I refused to act like it never happened. I was wrong, and I needed to be held accountable, or I would continue a course of destruction. As a parent, it was my responsibility to model and teach my girls how to respect themselves as well as others.

Lastly, in verse 7 of 1 Corinthians chapter 13, Paul explains, "Love protects the relationship when something (or someone) threatens to destroy it; trusts that Jesus will be able to help work things out; and holds fast to faith, principles, and priorities until the storm is over."

Understanding, teaching, and living these principles helped us keep our family balanced and healthy as the girls grew from children to teenagers to adults. But only time would tell if the cycle had truly been broken.

On Christmas Eve of 2020, my daughters, their husbands, our grandson, and our granddogs came to spend the night. We have a tradition of everyone being under the same roof on Christmas morning.

I got up around seven thirty Christmas morning and met my younger daughter, Eryn, my older son-in-law, Hunter, and grandson, Lincoln, in the living room. (Hunter is married to Eden.) My grandson, Lincoln, had not slept well, so they were occupying him while Eden got some more rest. Lincoln was playing in the walker Eden bought him for Christmas.

She and I had put it together before going to bed. He was loving his newfound freedom and had quickly mastered "walking."

Eryn, Hunter, and I were so excited. It was so much fun watching him grin and scoot from room to room. Within minutes, his accomplishments were on our social media stories. We played with him, fed him, and changed his diaper. When he appeared to be winding down, I wrapped him up and began rocking him to sleep.

I glanced up in time to see Eden walk into the room. She did not have her Christmas morning face on. In a second, the atmosphere in the living room bristled with her animosity. On her way from the guest bedroom to the living room, she passed the empty walker in the kitchen, and the position of the seat area tattled on the three of us. Eden had missed his first experience in it.

We felt horrible. We had acted without thinking, and she had every right to be upset. As she voiced her disappointment and anger, there was nothing we could do but apologize. All of us took responsibility for the action. Eden turned around and went back into her bedroom and shut the door.

Eryn, Hunter, and I sat in silence after her abrupt departure. I stared down at Lincoln as my mind went back to the countless ruined Christmases of my childhood. But, before I sank into a comfortable pity party, I whispered a prayer, asking God for help.

Within a few minutes, Eden came out again. She had regained her composure, and the Christmas festivities began. The cycle had been broken.

The rest of the day was fantastic. So wonderful was it that I hated to see the day end.

———————

Since that Christmas, we have spent two vacations traveling in a motor home. The first time, we toured for seven days. The second time was in 2021. All seven of us (Reagan was not born until two years later) spent fourteen days touring the west in a forty foot motor home. My family compared it to a two-week sleepover.

We returned home on a Friday evening, and after fourteen days of invading each other's space, we still held our Saturday morning breakfast tradition. And it was just as celebratory as ever.

The Word works. God's promises are true.

Philippians 4:6–7 says, "Be anxious for nothing, but in everything by prayer and supplication, with thanksgiving, let your requests be made known to God; and the peace of God, which surpasses all understanding, will guard your hearts and mind through Christ Jesus."

If you need peace in your mind, home, and life, ask God for help. Pray for wisdom. Ask Him to help you break the unhealthy cycle and start fresh.

Cycle-breakers become cycle-makers, creating new cycles for victorious living. What new cycles are you creating?

THE PLOT TWIST

God is too good to be unkind,
and He is too wise to be mistaken.
And when we cannot trace His hand,
we must trust His heart.
When you are so weak
that you cannot do much more than cry,
you coin diamonds with both your eyes.
The sweetest prayers God ever hears
are the groans and sighs
of those who have no hope
in anything but his love.

Charles Spurgeon

"When you call on me, when you come
and pray to me, I'll listen.
When you come looking for me, you'll find me.
Yes, when you get serious about finding me
and want it more than anything else,
I'll make sure you won't be disappointed."
God's Decree.
"I'll turn things around for you…
You can count on it"

(Jeremiah 29:12–14 MSG).

16

THE ABUSIVE GOD

So correct me, Lord, but please be gentle.
Do not correct me in anger, for I would die.
(Jeremiah 10:24 NLT)

We were in junior high when Dad taught us how long our skirts should be. We lived in a two-story house, and Trudy and I were downstairs, waiting on Jonette so we could walk to the bus stop together.

Dad had been in a mood all morning and we had been scurrying like mice, trying to finish getting ready while doing our best to avoid him.

Trudy and I froze as his heavy footsteps approached from the kitchen to where we stood. Jonette appeared at the top of the stairs and smiled as she glided down. She was a beauty. Everyone loved her.

As she neared the bottom, Dad commanded her to walk back up a few steps and stand still. Her panicked face mirrored ours. We had no clue what was about to happen, but we knew from his tone it wouldn't be pleasant. Dad returned with an ink pen and drew lines on Jonette's legs where her dress ended.

The pressure of his hand on the pen caused bruises and blood to appear almost simultaneously. With one fluid motion, he released the pen and pulled the belt from his pants. He had her stand still, holding her skirt up a few inches, while he used his belt to accent the marks made by the ink pen. She was screaming, and Trudy and I were silently crying, doing our best not to draw any attention to ourselves.

Dad ordered her to march up the stairs and find something long enough to cover those marks. He threatened to mark any of us who dared to show our knees in public, and we believed him. He may not have lived what he preached, but if he promised to whip us, he always carried out that promise.

———

I was twenty-four years old the last time Dad hit me.

I had finished college and was working full-time in my mother's accounting office. I heard the phone ring, and the secretary sent the call through to my mom, yelling that my dad was the caller.

My shoulders knotted up. His calls usually meant that he needed something. He rarely called just to see what she was doing. Sure enough, within minutes, Mom called me into her office. Dad had lost his wallet and she needed me to go help him look for it.

We seemed to spend a lot of time searching for something Dad had misplaced. Keys, wallets, his false teeth, important documents. Dad didn't have a system for important stuff. And when he needed it, the longer it took to find it, the angrier he became.

I dreaded having to be the one to go help him search. I prayed the entire way home, begging God to show me exactly where it was.

God did not.

Dad was already angry when I walked in the front door. He was late for some meeting and was positive someone had moved his wallet from his nightstand. He was convinced that we were all out to make his life miserable and said as much to me as I silently began scouring their bedroom.

I checked behind the bed, under the nightstand, the trash can, and the dresser, and although I had seen him checking his suit pockets, I thought I would double-check them before moving to another room.

I never saw his fist coming. I just felt the impact, and the force knocked me to the floor in a daze. I stared straight ahead, caught my breath, and remained motionless, my head resting on the carpet. I had stopped showing pain a long time ago.

He yelled for me to get up and informed me that if I looked in the same place more than once again, there was more from where that came from.

I was numb. I don't know that I hated him. I didn't feel anything for him.

We continued to comb the house before moving the search party to his vehicle. The wallet was on the floorboard of the front passenger side, buried beneath store receipts, newspapers, and Styrofoam cups stained with dark-roast Community Coffee.

During the five-minute drive back to the office, I examined my bruised jaw in the rearview mirror. I wanted revenge. But more than that, I wanted him out of my life. Forever.

I knew I would not miss him.

———

For over half of my life, I served an abusive God. Although I was raised in a pastor's home, never missed a service, and was constantly around the church, I was afraid of God. My obedience to His Word was not out of respect and love. I served Him out of fear of being punished.

Children get their perception of God from their relationship with their earthly father, therefore, my God was easily irritated, demanding, and required perfection. He waited for you to make a mistake, then judged harshly and carried out punishment swiftly. I did not just fear God, I was scared to death of Him.

Evangelists and guest speakers who came to our church during my childhood only confirmed my fears of God. They preached about judgment day often. We were repeatedly warned that only a few of us would make it into heaven. I was certain I would not be among the chosen few.

The rapture of the church was a scary, mystical event in which one out of every two people remained on the earth while the other soared blissfully into the sky to meet the Lord. The odds of me being the one soaring were not promising.

Some of the songs we sang in church sounded like death sentences. "Jesus is Coming Soon" was an up-tempo song about the soon return of Christ. We clapped our hands and smiled as we bellowed out that Jesus was soon to come at any time, and a lot of folks were doomed.

———

One female evangelist who frequented our church preached hell so hot we could almost feel it. She always ended her sermons with a song titled "Left Behind." The lyrics of the chorus created havoc on my abused and immature heart with implications that there was no hope and the odds of me being left behind were a real possibility.

Her soulful voice filled our small church and sent chills up my spine and ice through my veins. I cried each time she sang it. I knew I was doomed. But I still would go to the altar and plead for my life, knowing that it was probably a futile attempt.

Dad didn't want me. He didn't like me. And I was only one of five children he was responsible for. What were my odds with God, who had *billions* of children? Why would He be concerned with me when He had so many other more qualified children to choose from?

And did I mention God's anger issues? He didn't play.

Look at the book of Genesis for proof. Right away, we read how God gets so angry about the wickedness of humanity that He decides to "destroy all flesh in which is the breath of life; everything that is on the earth shall die" (Genesis 6:17 NASB). Soon afterward, God destroys the earth with a flood.

In Genesis 19: 24–25, "Then the Lord rained brimstone and fire on Sodom and Gomorrah... destroying the inhabitants and anything that grew on the ground."

My perception of God was reinforced as I read the stories about the wrath of God throughout the Old Testament. God struck Moses' sister, Miriam, with leprosy because she was jealous of her brother. The earth opened and swallowed rebellious Israelites. Plagues and sickness claimed the lives of hundreds who were disobedient.

This was a God I understood and fearfully served. I understood Him because my earthly father was just like Him.

As I studied the Word of God, viewing it through the lens of my earthly father, it only confirmed my suspicions. I would never be good enough.

In Leviticus, the twenty-first chapter, the Lord lays out the regulations for the conduct of a priest of the Old Testament. Of course, they were to be as sinless as possible. I expected that.

But when I got to verses 17 and 18, my heart sank. It read, "Speak to Aaron [Aaron was the first priest and it was prophesied that his descendants would be priests as well] saying, 'No man of your descendants in succeeding generations, who has **any defect**, may approach to offer the bread of his God. For any man who has a **defect** shall not approach; a man blind or lame, who has a **marred face.**'"

Verse 21 repeated the expectations: "No man of the descendants of Aaron the priest, who has a **defect**, shall come near to offer the offerings made by fire to the Lord. He has a **defect**; he shall not come near to offer the bread of his God" (NKJV).

I had a defect. God didn't want me near Him.

Not only was I not good enough to be a priest, but I was also not good enough to be a sacrifice. God required perfection in behavior and form. I had neither.

Repeatedly, in the Old Testament, God required sacrifices to cover the sins of the people. But every animal sacrificed had to be *without spot* or *without blemish*.

Leviticus 1:3 says, "If his offering is a burnt sacrifice of the herd, let him offer a male **without blemish**" (NKJV).

Numbers 19:2 repeats the requirement: "Speak unto the children of Israel, that they bring thee a red heifer **without spot**" (KJV).

Numbers 28:3 says, "And thou shalt say unto them, This is the offering made by fire which ye shall offer unto the Lord; two lambs of the first year **without spot** day by day, for a continual offering."

Those words, "without spot" and "without blemish," would glare at me from the pages of my Bible, reaffirming that I, covered with scars, was unacceptable in His sight.

I wasn't just physically covered with scars; I had made stupid choices that had left internal ugly scars as well. I could not conceive how anyone, especially our perfect God, could love me.

17

WHO IS GOD?

Looking back over my life, I caught glimpses of a God whose character I couldn't relate to and definitely didn't understand.

From the time I was twenty-two, my surgeries were performed in a Catholic hospital. After I'd been prepped for surgery, I would be taken to a holding room until the doctor was available. The medication to ease my anxiety caused me to be nauseated if I moved. So, I would lie as still as possible, staring straight ahead.

As I lay on the hospital gurney, I would stare at the ceiling, which was covered with Scriptures full of promises from a God I had never known.

One said, "Before I formed you in the womb, I knew you; Before you were born I sanctified you" (Jeremiah 1:5). I knew "sanctified" meant "consecrated or set apart." My cynical mind would think, "Yeah. You got that one right. You definitely set me apart and made me look different from everyone else!"

Another verse often displayed was Jeremiah 29:11, which reads, "For I know the thoughts [or the plans] that I think toward you, says the Lord, thoughts of peace and not of evil, to give you a future and a hope."

"Really?" I silently accused. "You thought THIS mess of my life was a GOOD PLAN?"

Then God blessed me with children. I remember anticipating each arrival. While I was pregnant, I dreamed of my life with them and worked for months preparing a place specifically for them. Clothes were bought, walls were painted, and the house was sanitized repeatedly. I wanted only the best for them.

I made a commitment to them long before I met them. I would always be their mother, and they would always be my child. Always.

I made sure they were dressed in the best I could afford. Their clothes were always cleaned and ironed, and their hair was always washed and fixed. I made sure that our home was the environment where they could mature into confident young women.

I was their mother, and I took pride in the way I took care of them.

One day it dawned on me that their well-being reflected how much I loved them. My reputation was at stake.

> **My distrust of God limited His influence in my life.**

It would have made me sad if they changed out of the clothes I provided and put on torn and tattered clothes, walking around looking homeless. I would have been angry if they needed something and did not ask me for help. I would have been mortified if they began worrying about paying our mortgage or begging for food on the street. I worked hard for them, and their contentment spoke volumes about my reputation as a parent.

Slowly, it began to sink in that my dad's behavior toward me was irrational. My relationship with my daughters was nothing like what I had experienced with my father. Their relationship with their father was nothing like I had ever seen. As I watched my children interact with their father, my view of my Heavenly Father began to change.

God created me. He formed me. He wanted what was best for me all along. I just kept taking detours from the path He had for me. My distrust of Him had limited His influence in my life.

As this revelation hit me, I felt like God spoke to me and said, *"My reputation was at stake before I formed you in the womb. That's why I immediately began making a plan for your life."*

Rereading the Bible with this new filter (view of God) made things a whole lot clearer.

The laws in the Old Testament were not written to keep the Israelites from having fun. They were a blueprint for longevity on this earth. The laws were the reason the Israelites multiplied into such a strong, healthy nation.

The Ten Commandments were not written to control the people. They were given to establish a civilized society. The Israelites were God's children, and His reputation was at stake.

As a mom, I did my best to teach Eden and Eryn the principles from the Word of God. I also taught them Paula's principles of how to keep a room clean and how to behave in public and dress modestly. When they obeyed these principles, my reputation improved.

When they chose not to, they were disciplined. It wasn't because I hated them. It was because I wanted them to succeed. I built my reputation by taking care of them. They protected my reputation by how they responded to that care.

At the time, my girls didn't think the spankings or punishments were for their own good. When they got older, they told me that when I spanked them, it didn't hurt at all. In fact, when they were in trouble, and both knew they would get a spanking, Eden would tell Eryn, "Cry like it hurts, and she will stop."

Because I had a relationship with them, they knew I would not hurt them.

———

Eryn began attending preschool when she turned three years old. A few months into the program, I received a phone call from her teacher. My eyes widened when she told me, "Eryn is crying and saying she wants you to come to the school and whip her."

I was as confused as the teachers were at Eryn's request but hurried to meet with them. When I pulled up, Eryn's teacher was standing outside of the door with Eryn, who was indeed crying. As I approached, Eryn wailed, "I want you to whip me!"

I could feel my face turning red as I swore that I had no clue why she would be saying that.

She rarely got spankings. She didn't need them. She was a good kid.

The teacher left us, and Eryn and I sat outside and talked until she calmed down. A few minutes later, Eryn was ready to join her class, and I went back to work.

A few days later, the same thing happened again. The teacher called to report that Eryn wanted me to come to the school and give her a spanking. When I got to the classroom, I was still as clueless as before and even more embarrassed.

"I'm not sure why she is saying this. I promise that I do not abuse my kids. And if I did, why would she be asking for it?"

Again, Eryn and I sat in my car. I waited for her to calm down and then began to question her. When she finally explained the scenario, I had a revelation.

One of her classmates had done something wrong and the teacher had disciplined the child with words and administered a short spanking. Her classmate had screamed and cried, and Eryn was traumatized.

So, every time the teacher corrected Eryn, Eryn became fearful of getting a spanking from her, and decided she wanted me to come and spank her instead of taking her chances with the teacher.

Thank God we figured that out before child services had to get involved!

This was my revelation: because of our relationship, she trusted my discipline above anyone else's.

This was the relationship I needed to develop with God.

Jeremiah 30:11 says, "For I am with you and will save you, says the Lord…I will not completely destroy you. I will discipline you, but with justice; I cannot let you go unpunished" (NIV)

Punishment without love is abuse.

King David, the man after God's own heart, had that kind of relationship with God. He was aware of God's reputation when it came to administering punishment.

Relying on the strength of his army instead of the strength of his God, David numbered the valiant men in Israel and Judah. He knew he had sinned, and punishment was imminent. A prophet was sent to David, and he presented to David three possible consequences from which to choose.

2 Samuel 24:14 gives us David's response based on his relationship with God.

"I am in great distress. Please let us fall into the hand of the Lord, for His mercies are great; but do not let me fall into the hand of man!" (NKJV)

If the children of Israel had understood the importance of the reputation of God, they could have saved themselves forty years of wandering through the wilderness.

———

When God decided to deliver the children of Israel out of Egypt, He sent a murderer with a speech impediment to lead them out. Even I could have come up with a better plan than that.

According to Exodus 12:37 (NKJV), "...about 600,000 men on foot, besides children..." were delivered from Egypt in one night. When the Egyptian army pursued them, the Angel of God, who went before the camp of Israel, moved and went behind them; and the pillar of cloud came between the camp of the Egyptians and the camp of Israel so that "it was a cloud and darkness to the one, and it gave light by night to the other" (Exodus 14:20).

This is the God we serve; to one, He gives darkness, and by the same action, He gives light to another.

During their journey through the wilderness, God covered them with a cloud by day, blocking the sun. Temperatures in the wilderness could easily reach over 120°. At night, He covered them with fire. The temperature at night could dip below 40°.

It is my opinion that God didn't do those things (cloud and fire) just for protection. I believe that it was also because He wanted to get as close to them as possible.

When they became hungry, He rained down manna from heaven. When they were thirsty, water came from a rock. Anything they needed, God provided. His reputation was on the line!

With all these visible miracles, they viewed God through the lens of the abuse heaped on them by the Egyptian government. He became a God who withheld from them and sought opportunities to reprimand them.

This was the same God I served for over half of my life. I had a skewed view and questioned God's motives because of it.

When they murmured and complained, God got angry. During those times of anger, Moses would remind God of His reputation. In Exodus 32:11, "Moses pleaded with the Lord…and said, 'Lord, why does Your wrath burn hot against your people whom You have brought out of the land of Egypt with great power and with a mighty hand? Why should the Egyptians speak, and say, "He brought them out to harm them, to kill them in the mountains, and to consume them from the face of the earth?"'" (NKJV)

In other words, Moses was warning God that the Egyptians were going to talk bad about Him.

Moses asked God to turn from His fierce anger and relent from harming the people. Verse 14 says, "So the Lord relented from the harm which he said he would do to his people."

Finally! A God I could serve without being scared. A God who could be reasoned with. A God I could have faith in. A God who kept His Word. But most of all, a God who took pride in how He treated His people.

I had viewed Him as an abusive parent for far too long. My "time in the wilderness" could have been shortened if I had understood His reputation.

When my father raised his arm, it was often to inflict pain on whoever was nearby. We would shrink back, begging for mercy. God is not waiting for me to mess up so that He can punish me. His arms are not held out to strike me when I fail. That was my earthly father's reputation.

God's arms are outstretched to catch me when I fall. He makes the landing as soft as possible. He *loves* me. It is a love that took me years to understand. I had never seen a love like that displayed toward me by an earthly father, so I never believed I could have it from a Heavenly One.

What do you believe? What is the record on repeat in your thoughts? Could you, too, have a skewed view of the God that loves you?

18

THE LOVING GOD

In 2011, my oldest sister, Jonette, called with the news that Dad had been diagnosed with non-Hodgkin's lymphoma. I processed the reality that the chances of developing a relationship with him now had a shorter timeline.

I asked that she let me know when his chemotherapy would begin. I knew the first week following treatment would be the best time to visit him, as the effects of the harsh drugs would be delayed a few days.

He lived over two and a half hours away, and I set aside a full day to drive there, spend time with him, and return by nightfall. The first couple of times, one or two of my sisters accompanied me. The third time, Cliff was my chauffeur. Dad enjoyed the attention, and I was hopeful that we would form a bond.

In between visits, I made it a point to call him at least once a week for an update. His inconsistent demeanor upon answering created anxiety for me. He would either answer in a cheerful tone or greet me angrily, letting me know that I had woken him. My heart beat harder and faster each time I waited for him to respond to my call. One day, he picked up the phone, angrily announced that I had once again awakened him, and slammed the phone down without saying "Goodbye."

I excused his behavior, telling myself that it was the effects of the medication causing such a violent reaction. I called the next week, and he hung up on me again. Only this time, he didn't speak at all. I believed it was due to poor phone reception and would try again the next day.

That afternoon, I received a call from Jonette, and before I could utter more than a "Hello," she warned, "Do not call Dad anymore!"

Confused at her request, I asked what she meant. She explained that she had just hung up on Dad because he was bragging to her about hanging up on me.

I was dumbfounded and crushed. Did he really hate me so much he couldn't tolerate my voice on the phone? If he couldn't take my phone calls, I certainly was not going to subject myself to being rejected face-to-face.

I never visited him again.

But the guilt of not calling or visiting my dying father weighed heavily on me. I prayed for him every day and asked God for guidance to help soften my father's heart. God deposited the idea of sending him a handwritten card. For the remainder of Dad's life, I sent a heartfelt message to him weekly. He never responded. I don't know if he read them, threw them away, or burned them. I didn't ask.

I would mourn the loss of the possibility of a relationship with him when he died, but I would not feel guilty. I knew I had done my part.

Dad had a problem, and it wasn't me.

For the past three-plus decades, I've been privileged to have a front-row seat to a healthy father/child relationship. From the moment Eden and Eryn entered this world, Clifton was attentive to their needs. He was in the room when they took their first breath, and, in that instant, he became willing to die for them.

I observed him more than once, holding them and staring at them with tears in his eyes while they slept. They kept us up at night. Diapers, baby formula, and doctor's appointments drained our bank accounts. After their arrival, "family time" replaced "free time," and he was intentional about it.

He loved them because they existed. Period.

He did his best not to miss doctor appointments, first days of school, field trips, awards ceremonies, etc. He even officiated at the funeral of their goldfish, Splash. If it was important to them, it was important to him.

When a doctor's visit required an injection, they cried, and he cried with them. His face would be as red as theirs when we waded through the packed waiting room as we exited the office.

When actions or attitudes required an "adjustment," he dreaded having to be the disciplinarian. He would put on a brave face, explain why they were being spanked, administer the punishment, and go to another room to cry.

Cliff would wait as long as he could before he hurried back into their room to sit on their bed and cry with them. Although he knew it was necessary, he hated it.

Long before they were teenagers, spankings were no longer necessary. Their relationship with him was such that they broke at the thought of disappointing him. When rules had to be given after a driver's license was obtained, they didn't obey for fear of punishment. They were confident that any restriction was out of concern for their well-being.

It was during their teenage years that Clifton truly taught me how God feels about His children.

Our younger daughter was sixteen and very involved in school activities. It was normal for her to stay after school to work on projects or upcoming events, come home to eat supper, and return to the school to work some more.

One Thursday evening, she came in from school just in time to eat with the family and announced that she had to return to help a teacher complete a project. We agreed and after we finished eating, we cleaned the kitchen, and she waved as she headed out the door.

Our older daughter, Eden, had asked if she could go over to a friend's house to play games, and she followed Eryn out of the kitchen door. It was November, and the sun had gone to sleep while we sat at the table. I stood and watched until I could no longer see their taillights and prayed a familiar prayer, "God, protect my girls until they return."

The house was unusually quiet as Clifton worked on his laptop in our bedroom, and I sat on a barstool at the kitchen island and worked on balancing a checkbook. While I was concentrating on finding an error, God spoke clearly into the quiet, "Eryn is not where she said she was."

I picked up my phone and called Eryn's. It rang three or four times before switching over to voicemail. The hair on the back of my neck stood at attention as I responded to God's voice and hurried through the house to find Cliff.

My voice disguised my emotions as I announced, "Eryn is not at the school. I need you to go and check on her."

Cliff looked at me, confused, and asked, "How do you know?"

Without hesitation, I replied, "I don't know how I know. I just do."

Praying that I was wrong, I busied myself with laundry while Clifton drove the short distance to the high school. My phone rang in less than two minutes. It was Cliff reporting that her vehicle was the only one at the school, and he didn't see any lights on inside the building.

Within seconds, I was in my vehicle and racing to the school. She had never lied to us before.

Where could she be? Was someone holding her hostage? Had she been kidnapped?

I tried to find her phone by using our Life 360 app, but the location service had been turned off.

As I approached the building, I could see Clifton running from door to door, pulling on the handles and beating on the glass. He stopped at windows to see if any were unlocked. After circling the entire building, he began looking for something to break the glass on the front door. As he approached it, he saw someone at the end of a long hallway. He began beating as hard as he could and screaming at the top of his lungs.

A custodian hesitantly approached the glass doors and spoke without opening, "What do you want?"

"My daughter is in there!" Cliff shouted.

The man replied, "There's no one here except for me."

Recognizing Clifton from the community and realizing his desperation, the custodian allowed Cliff in the building. I watched from the front of the building as Clifton raced down the hall. He opened every door in search of his baby girl. I knew no room would be missed.

When he ran out of the building, his eyes mirrored the fear in my own. I continued dialing her number and took my first deep breath in what felt like hours when I heard her voice on the other end.

"Where are you?" Cliff questioned.

She gave the name of a classmate who lived less than a mile from the school. Cliff broke speed limits and ran stop signs, anxious to get to her. The girl's mother met him at the back door. Eryn was not there.

It felt as though we were living a nightmare. Only we couldn't wake up. The night air was chilly yet sweat poured from both of our faces. This time, Clifton called from his phone, and she answered on the first ring.

"Tell me where you are."

This time she told the truth.

I witnessed the look of relief when he heard her voice. She was alive. She had lied and deceived us, but it did not stop him from searching for her until he found her. The consequences of her actions did not include verbal or physical abuse.

She was not a disappointment. She was his child.

———

In 2016, one of the elementary schools in our town received a phone call from a person threatening to harm the students and staff. My daughter Eden worked at that school, and the student of that parent was in her classroom.

Eden sent text messages to Cliff and me, asking for prayer. We prayed as we raced to our vehicle and drove like car thieves toward the school.

As soon as Eden saw her father, she was relieved. The threat of danger still hung in the air, but Dad was on the scene. His presence was all she needed to continue being the voice of comfort to her students. Once Dad arrived, his reputation as a father was at stake. She knew that if Dad was there, nothing would happen to her that he could prevent.

———

I got a glimpse of that kind of father just once, that I can remember.

It was a hot, humid summer afternoon, and we were at my grandmother's house in Evangeline. Days of torrential rain had created a flood, and her house was inaccessible except by boat.

Maw-Maw Lormand insisted on staying in her house to protect it. So, day after day, Dad would pull his boat behind his van and park along the highway. We would load the boat with supplies and make the trek through the marsh to Grandma's house.

After unloading the supplies and helping Grandma put them away, we were allowed to fish from the porch or paddle the canoe around her yard. Dad didn't act up around Grandma. She would have been quick to scold him.

Being around so much water must have shrunk my bladder because it seemed I had to go every few minutes. The only bathroom in the house was downstairs, and you had to walk through Grandma's bedroom to get to it.

As I cleared the doorway of the bathroom, I heard Dad's boots hitting the wooden floor just behind me. The way he said my name caused my blood to turn cold, and I froze. Just in front of me was the sink and above it, a mirrored medicine cabinet. I saw my reflection as well as the familiar angry look on my dad's face. Thoughts raced through my mind, *What did*

I do wrong this time? Was I going to the bathroom too often? Was grandma upset that I used too much toilet paper?"

His voice continued in that tone: "Stand right there and don't move an inch until I come back!"

I stood terrified as I heard his boots retreat out of the bedroom and the screen door hinges squeaked his departure through the back door.

What is he going to get to beat me with? He had his belt on. Why hadn't he used that?

I knew better than to move. If Dad said not to move an inch, he'd check when he got back and know if I had.

I never heard Dad come back in. As I stood facing the sink, I watched in horror as he raised a shovel he held with both of his hands and thrust it swiftly toward the back of my feet. The loud thud caused me to scream and jump simultaneously involuntarily.

When I didn't feel any pain, I turned around to see what Dad had hit with the shovel, and there, cut in half, was a two-foot-long water moccasin.

I had no idea that a poisonous snake had escaped the murky waters beneath the house and was poised to strike. Had I not been obedient, had I moved just one inch, I would have gotten bit and probably died. With the flooding, it would have taken too long to get me to a hospital.

Sweat mixed with tears ran down my face. I realized that this time, Dad's instructions were for my salvation, not my damnation.

For such a long time, I viewed God as the maker of an endless list of rules and laws, handing down punishments and sentences when those laws were broken.

Over time, I understood that He was more than that. Although I still viewed Him as a distant figure, I saw that He was doing His best to care for, protect, and ensure that His people were successful. When I reread the Bible through the lens of His love, I became aware of how much He wanted to change our perception of His reputation.

As I read about His birth, my view of Him began to change. God robed Himself in flesh and came to us in the form of a baby. Scholars were awaiting a king accompanied by a vast army. But He appeared as a helpless, innocent child, totally dependent on others for His care.

The God who demanded perfection was born in an unclean stable. It wasn't because He was poor. Scriptures prove quite the opposite. Joseph and Mary were in Bethlehem to pay taxes. They didn't lack money.

Secondly, the reason He was born in the stable was clearly stated in Luke 2:7, "…because there was no room for them in the inn" (NKJV).

Joseph and Mary were very capable of paying for a room. Being born in a stable was God's choice.

When Jesus began His public ministry, He did not follow Jewish protocol. He didn't head to the synagogue in search of followers, He went to the seashore. His invitation was extended to fishermen first, men who weren't afraid of taking risks and were used to hard work. They were dirty, smelly, and uncultured—the complete opposite of who the "church" would have considered for such a task.

Later, He headed to the tax office to recruit His next disciple (Matthew 9:9 NKJV). Tax collectors were hated by the people. They were known for extortion, demanding more money than was owed for taxes and pocketing the difference. They had their own category of evil. There were "taxpayers," and there were "sinners."

Many more than Matthew must have followed Jesus because verse 10 says that as Jesus sat at the table in the house, **many** tax collectors and sinners came and sat down with Him.

The perfection-seeking God was sharing a meal with imperfect, immoral people, and it angered the rulers of the church. The Pharisees knew that "holy" people did not socialize with "unholy" people. They made it their mission to make sure He followed the rules. But Jesus stuck to His mission, to change the world's perception of His reputation.

The law was written for the preservation of humanity. The law stated that people with sores, bleeding, leprosy, and anything that looked sickly were deemed unclean. They were unfit for society, and anyone or anything that touched them was unclean too.

One day, after preaching a lengthy sermon on a mountain, which Matthew covers in chapters 5–7 of his book, Jesus is trying to leave, but the congregation is following Him. As they watched in horror, a leper stopped the procession by worshiping Him, saying, "Lord, if You are willing, You can make me clean" (Matthew 8:2).

Then Jesus did the unexpected. He reached out and **touched** the leper, then said, "I am willing; be cleansed."

Not only was Jesus willing to make the leprous man clean, but He was also willing to touch him. Because of the restrictions of the law, it was probably the first human touch the man had experienced since his diagnosis.

As I read that passage, I thought about how many times I had felt unclean, an outcast of society. And how many times I had felt like everyone was staring and judging me as God did, deeming me unworthy. Too many to remember.

This was my own perception because I did not understand the love of God. He is not repulsed by our imperfections. He is willing to touch us and make us whole.

———

Another one of my favorite stories is the woman with the issue of blood. According to the law, if she was bleeding, if she had a blood disorder of some kind, she was to remain quarantined until the bleeding stopped.

At one time, she had money. At one time, she felt good. But sickness had drained her of her income, her friends, and her status in the community. Somehow rumors of Jesus' miracles reached her in her isolated state. Desperate for a change, she sought out Jesus Christ.

Knowing the law, she didn't want to draw attention to herself. She would have been in so much trouble with the rulers of the church if they knew she was in public in her condition. Seeing the crowd surrounding Him, she decided that if she could secretly touch the hem of His garment, He wouldn't know she touched Him. Her faith said, "If I can just touch something connected to Him, I can be made whole!" (Mark 5:28 PKLV)

As she reached out and touched Him, Jesus felt healing virtue flow and asked, "Who touched My clothes?" (Mark 5:30 NKJV) I want to point out that Jesus *felt* her *faith*. She was terrified and wasn't admitting anything. But neither did she run away.

She paused long enough for the disciples to become irritated. They responded (Mark 5:31 PKLV), "What are you talking about? There are people everywhere pushing against you and *touching* You. And You want us to point out *one person* who touched You?"

Luke recounts the same story in chapter 8:47 NKJV: "Now when the woman saw that she was not hidden, she came trembling; and falling down before Him, she declared to Him in the presence of all the people, the reason she had touched Him and how she was healed immediately."

She had to confess the sin she had committed. She, who was unclean, had touched Him and made Him unclean.

Instead of quoting the law and demanding consequences, Jesus responded, "Daughter, be of good cheer." She should have already been cheerful. She was healed. Twelve years of misery, twelve years of isolation, lonely birthdays, and holidays celebrated alone all came to an end! But I believe He said this because the same way He felt her faith when she reached out, He now felt her fear of the imminent judgment for what she had done.

But no judgment came. Jesus released her as He said, "Your faith has made you well. Go in peace."

What I discovered through these stories was that God was nothing like my earthly father. God is not repulsed by our scars, our sickness, or our past mistakes. He won't ignore us or hang up on us when we reach out to Him. He longs to interact with us and change our perception of His reputation.

After Mom died, I started seeing a counselor. I thought it was to help me deal with the death of her and my father. My parents died within five months of each other.

Dad's death took with it all hopes of having a "normal" relationship between a father and daughter. Mom's death created a void that had been filled with daily conversations combined with consistent manipulation. She refused to allow me to set and keep boundaries that would protect myself and my family.

It's family. You have to forgive and forget. Families stay together.

Her definition of forgiving was to ignore the behavior and allow it to continue.

Interactions with either of them left me feeling the weight of guilt, although I never knew exactly what I had done wrong.

It took months to work through all that was wrong with me.

Yes, you read that right, *with me.*

During one of those sessions, I discovered how much bitterness and anger I was hanging on to. It was my job to get rid of it.

I remember sitting across from an empty chair and forgiving my parents for years of ruined holidays, birthdays, and other celebratory moments Those special days were ruined by the turmoil created by them because they chose not to control their emotions.

One such instance was the day I graduated from college. Dad had insisted that we all ride together to the ceremony. He complained the entire way there because of how early I had to be present. I was inconveniencing the whole family.

Afterward, my dad threatened to make me walk home if I did not go to the car immediately. He had more important things to do than stand around watching me tell my friends goodbye. He ranted the duration of the thirty-minute ride back to our house, angry about the length of the commencement. I held my emotions in check. He would not know how hurt I was.

But during counseling, I did not hold back. Sobbing to the point of being incoherent, I voiced my resentment for not having a childhood. I was fifty-one years old, and I did not know how to play. I did not know how to relax and enjoy periods of "not working" without feeling guilty.

During those sessions, I "let go of bitterness, rage, and anger" (Ephesians 4:31 NKJV), and healing began. Those old, thick, internal scars were cut away, and smooth ones began to form. God began to replace those terrible memories with peaceful, joyful new ones.

———

Saturday morning brunch began when the girls were very young. It took on an air of festivity as they reached adulthood. When Eden began dating Hunter exclusively, he was added to the weekly celebration. When Eryn introduced Jacob to the family, we had to replace our four-seater kitchen table with a table for six.

Both girls are married, and two grandsons, Lincoln and Reagan, have been delightful additions. Although we all live in the same neighborhood and talk almost daily, Saturday morning brunch is still a weekly occurrence. The celebration often lasts two or more hours.

Over the past ten years, God has re-paid every stolen holiday, with interest.

There are Saturdays when I get up early and spend time with God before my family arrives. As I spend time thanking Him for the day, anticipating the arrival of my kids and grandkids, my heart is so full of peace and joy that it gushes from my tear ducts.

I challenge you to get to know the God who created you. The God who knows the thoughts and intents of your heart. The God who knows the number of hairs on your head. The God who thrives on your faith in His reputation.

The Loving God.

"But if you pray to God and seek the favor of the Almighty,
and if you are pure and live with integrity,
he will surely rise up and restore your happy home.
And though you started out with little,
you will end with much" Job 8:5–8 NLT.

Flipping your script may seem daunting, but remember, God holds your rewrite pen with a steady hand.

CREDITS

Eden and Eryn - Thank you for letting me grow up with you. You have been my loudest and proudest cheerleaders. Your smiles still take my breath away.

Hunter and Jacob - You were designed by descriptive prayer. God checked off each box and sent you to our family. Your love for God and my girls is unwavering.

Lincoln and Reagan - Clifton refers to you both as "Medicine." It doesn't matter what is going on in our world, seeing you makes everything better. Thankfully, you live next door, and we are able to get a "dose" of you often.

To my sisters - Thank you for sharing and validating the stories in this book. You've been my advocates and inspiration for as long as I can remember. The greatest gift Mom and Dad gave me was you.

To my JWC family - Thank you for letting me practice speaking in front of you and for asking for my notes after. You made me realize I had written something worth reading.

To Natalie & Chermaine - Thank you for your relentless work to turn my dream into a reality. You've both become family by choice.

To Called Creatives Leaders, Lisa Whittle & Alli Worthington - Thank you for explaining the level of difficulty, equipping me with the tools, and encouraging me to pursue my calling.

ABOUT THE AUTHOR

 Jennings, Louisiana is where Paula LeJeune calls home. A graduate of Welsh High School, she earned her Bachelor of Science in Accounting from McNeese State University.

Married to Clifton for more than 35 years, Paula has devoted over 29 years, alongside her husband, to pastoring the Jesus Worship Center. Paula finds great joy in her family, serving as a loving mother to Eden LeJeune Self (Hunter) and Eryn LeJeune Davis (Jacob), and as "Grancy" to Lincoln and Reagan.

Committed to her community, she currently represents on the Jefferson Davis Parish School Board and previously served as chaplain for the Jefferson Davis chapter of the National Federation of Republican Women.

Perfectly Imperfect is Paula's second book. Drawing loosely from her life experiences, Paula's initial foray into writing is a children's book on self-esteem building titled, *The Perfectly Imperfect Princess: An Un-fairy Tale Gone Right.*

Her desire to see others flourish has taken her across the nation, where she shares her insights on faith, relationships, and leadership at churches, marriage seminars, and women's conferences, leaving a lasting impact on audiences everywhere.

If you find a good shoe sale, you can let Paula know on Facebook and Instagram (@PaulaLeJeune). Or feel free to email her publisher; she's sure they won't mind.

ALSO FROM
PAULA LEJEUNE

Join Paula LeJeune on an inspiring journey through this captivating children's book. Based on her real life story, it's filled with hope for kids who feel life has been unfair.

Paula tours libraries and various venues to share her tale of bravery and optimism with children and young teens. She engages them through readings and interactive sessions, encouraging questions and discussions.

Help a child discover how even the toughest beginnings don't have to stay that way. Paula's books are available in paperback from Amazon or hardcover by emailing her at publications@thepeoplemover.org.

NOTES

Preview

1. Oxford English Dictionary, 2016: online

Chapter 3: Choosing to Live

1. Ibe, Uche. n.d. Making Music Magazine. Accessed February 3, 2024. https://makingmusicmag. com/three-ways-singing-makes-you-healthier/.

2. Young, Sarah. 2004. *Jesus Calling*. Nashville: Thomas Nelson.

3. Stanley, Andy. 2011. *Enemies of the Heart*. New York: Multnomah.

Chapter 6: Facing the Future

1. Leaf, Caroline. 2019. 21-Day Brain Detox. Accessed February 3, 2024. https://www.youtube.com/.

Chapter 12: Unashamed

1. Zehr, E. Paul. 2023. *Psychology Today.* 7 October. Accessed February 3, 2024. https://www.psychologytoday.com/us/blog/black-belt-brain/202310/sticks-and-stones-break-your-bones-but-words-hurt-your-brain.

2. Foy, Terri Savelle. 2020. *YouTube - Terri Savelle Foy.* 30 June. Accessed 2020. https://www.youtube.com/watch?v=NTuSGfMsKR0.

3. Groeschel, Craig. n.d. "Craig Groeschel Leadership Podcast." https://www.craiggroeschel.com/leadershippodcast.

Chapter 14: Creating Chaos

1. Martin, Sharon. 2021. *Live Well With Sharon Martin.* 24 June. Accessed February 20, 2024. https://www.livewellwithsharonmartin.com/we-repeat-what-we-dont-repair/.

Chapter 15: Redefining Chaos

1. Rohn, Jim. 2021. "Jim Rohn Talks Podcast."